10X Your Health

In 10 Minutes A Day

Unearth the Power of Grounding, Early Morning Sunshine, and Deep Breathing for Lifelong Wellbeing

Adrian Davis

British Library cataloguing in the publication data is available.

ISBN: 978-1-916720-13-8

As you turn each page, know that you're not just reading—you're taking actionable steps toward a life of immeasurable richness and well-being. The power to transform, to soar, and to achieve your greatest potential is within your grasp.

TABLE OF CONTENTS

INTRODUCTION

Welcome to a Transformative Journey Toward Better Health and Lifelong Well-being

In today's fast-paced world, it's easy to get caught in the whirlwind of responsibilities, deadlines, and endless to-do lists. The cumulative effect? Skyrocketing stress levels that take a heavy toll on our overall well-being. With our attention pulled in a million different directions, it's easy to overlook the one investment that yields the most significant returns: our health.

But let's get something straight—this isn't just about avoiding the flu next winter or squeezing in a temporary energy boost to make it through a grueling workday. No, the stakes are much higher. We're talking about the quality of your life. We're talking about a transformative journey toward a state of well-being that allows you to flourish—physically, mentally, and emotionally.

Imagine waking up each day with a sense of vitality, your body free from nagging aches and pains, your mind sharp, and your spirit uplifted. Imagine what it would be like to move through your day with a stable, enduring energy that empowers you to live more and achieve more. These aren't lofty dreams; they are entirely achievable goals.

We often think of well-being as a complicated puzzle, one that requires us to juggle gym memberships, specialized diets, and an arsenal of expensive supplements. But what if I told you that the key to unlocking this elevated state of health could be as simple as dedicating just 10 minutes of your day to practices that are grounded in scientific evidence and thousands of years of human experience?

Yes, you read that right—just 10 minutes a day to embark on a transformative journey toward better health and lifelong well-being.

So here you are, standing at the threshold of an empowering adventure. Are you ready to step across? Your path to a healthier, happier you starts right here, right now.

In this book, "10 X Your Health in 10 Minutes a Day," we aim to offer you an accessible, time-efficient, and highly effective roadmap to unlock a new level of health and vitality. We will delve into three core pillars—Grounding, Early Morning Sunshine, and Deep Breathing—each backed by scientific evidence and geared towards creating tangible improvements in your life. Through this approach, we provide a comprehensive yet remarkably simple guide that can truly make a difference—all in just 10 minutes a day.

So let's embark on this empowering journey together. Your path to a healthier, happier you starts now.

Why 10 Minutes a Day Matters

The Power of Small, Consistent Actions: How Just 10 Minutes a Day Can Transform Your Life

You might read the headline and think, "Can 10 minutes a day really make a difference in my health?" The answer is a resounding yes, and the secret lies in the incredible power of small, consistent actions. The notion that monumental changes require monumental efforts is a myth that has been debunked time and time again. In fact, significant transformation often comes from the steady accumulation of small efforts, applied consistently over time.

Consider the concept of compound interest, a principle often used in finance. When you invest a small amount of money consistently, over time, that sum grows exponentially thanks to the interest that accrues and then compounds. The same principle can be applied to your health and well-being. When you invest just 10 minutes a day in targeted, health-boosting activities, the 'interest' you earn is in the form of improved physical and mental health, better sleep, reduced stress, and an overall increase in well-being. Just like financial growth in compound interest, the 'health interest' accrues and compounds over time, leading to exponential benefits.

Think of it as a 'health snowball.' The first few times you roll it along, the changes are subtle—almost imperceptible. You might even question whether it's worth continuing. But every time you add that 10-minute layer—be it through grounding, soaking in the morning sun, or practicing deep breathing—your 'health snowball' grows larger and gathers momentum. Soon, the results become visible, tangible, and undeniable.

You'll start to see how these individual 10-minute efforts connect and interact, creating a synergistic effect that is far greater than the sum of its parts. Each daily ritual supports and amplifies the others, initiating a ripple effect of positive changes that extends into all areas of your life. Your focus sharpens; your energy levels rise; your sleep deepens; your stress diminishes.

It's important to stress that the power of this approach comes not from the intensity of the effort but from its consistency. Skipping a day won't result in immediate decline, just as a single day's effort won't produce a miraculous transformation. But a steady, unbroken string of these 10-minute investments? That's where the magic happens. And the best part? Anyone can do it. There are no barriers to entry, no special skills required, and no significant time commitments. It's a universally accessible strategy that places the potential for profound change firmly within everyone's grasp.

So if you're skeptical that just 10 minutes a day can make a meaningful difference, I invite you to put this theory to the test. Experience the transformative potential of small, consistent actions, and join the many who have already discovered that little changes can indeed lead to big results.

Real-Life Testimonies: The Transformative Power of 10 Minutes a Day

Sometimes, abstract ideas and scientific studies can feel distant and impersonal. That's why real-life stories of transformation can be so compelling; they provide concrete examples that these concepts genuinely work. Take the stories of Sarah and Mark, two individuals who have experienced firsthand the transformative impact of dedicating just 10 minutes a day to specific health-promoting activities.

Sarah's Journey to a Calmer Self

Sarah was like many of us—a busy professional juggling work, family, and an ever-growing list of responsibilities. Stress was her constant companion, and despite her best efforts, it began to take a toll on her health and well-being. A friend recommended incorporating deep breathing exercises into her daily routine. Skeptical but willing to try, Sarah committed to just 10 minutes each morning for this practice.

The change was almost immediate. Within a week, Sarah reported that her stress levels had noticeably decreased, and she felt more centered and calm throughout her day. It was as though those 10 minutes of focused breathing provided her with a kind of emotional and mental armor, enabling her to face the challenges of her day with more resilience and equanimity. The best part? This wasn't a one-time event but a lasting transformation. Sarah continues her 10-minute morning ritual to this day and has even added other healthy habits to her routine.

Mark Discovers the Power of Morning Sunshine

Mark had always been a night owl, which, over time, began to affect his mood and sleep quality. Then he read about the benefits of morning sunshine—how it can regulate circadian rhythms, improve mood, and even help with better sleep. Intrigued, Mark decided to give it a go. Each morning, he would spend 10 minutes sitting on his porch, sipping his coffee while soaking in the natural sunlight.

Within a month, the changes were undeniable. Mark reported feeling happier and more energetic during the day, and he started to experience a more consistent and restful sleep pattern. Those 10 minutes of morning sunshine had a ripple effect, influencing various aspects of his well-being.

The Takeaway

Sarah and Mark are not anomalies; they are living testimonials to the transformative potential of dedicating a mere 10 minutes a day to your well-being. Their experiences underscore the concept that small, consistent actions can yield significant results. By making a modest time investment each day, they changed the trajectory of their health and quality of life in meaningful ways. And if Sarah and Mark can do it, so can you. Their stories serve as inspiration and proof that you don't need to overhaul your entire life to experience the benefits of better health. You just need to start, and as they've shown, 10 minutes a day is enough to set you on a path to transformation.

The Science Behind the 10-Minute Focus: A Closer Look at the Data

While anecdotal evidence and personal testimonies offer compelling proof of the impact of a 10-minute daily routine, it's also important to ground these claims in scientific data. A growing body of research supports the idea that dedicating a small amount of time to specific activities can yield significant health benefits. Let's delve into some of the key studies that validate the importance of the 10-minute focus for better health.

Cardiovascular Health: A 10-Minute Brisk Walk

One compelling study, published in the Journal of the American Heart Association, specifically addresses the impact of short bursts of physical activity on cardiovascular health. The study found that even a mere 10-minute brisk walk could lead to measurable improvements in cardiovascular health. These benefits include lower blood pressure, reduced cholesterol levels, and improved blood circulation. The results are significant because they challenge the traditional belief that only extended periods of exercise can be beneficial for heart health. In this case, a short, consistent commitment—just 10 minutes a day—can make a substantial difference.

Stress Reduction: 10 Minutes of Mindfulness Meditation

Another groundbreaking study, published in the Journal of Clinical Psychology, explores the role of mindfulness meditation in stress reduction. The research found that just 10 minutes of mindfulness meditation daily led to a significant reduction in stress levels among participants. This is a crucial finding given that stress is often the root cause of various mental and physical health issues, including anxiety, depression, and even chronic diseases like heart problems and diabetes. By dedicating just 10 minutes a day to mindfulness, you can arm yourself with a potent tool to combat stress.

The Cumulative Effect: Why Consistency Matters

It's worth noting that these benefits are not just one-off events; they tend to be cumulative, compounding over time. The studies emphasize the importance of consistency—small, dedicated efforts made day in and day out. In a way, this validates the idea of a "ripple effect," where a minor but consistent commitment can lead to larger, long-term gains.

Conclusions from the Data

The message from these studies is unequivocal: A small amount of dedicated time can yield big health benefits. This isn't a speculative claim but a fact backed by rigorous scientific research. So whether it's a 10-minute brisk walk for cardiovascular health or a 10-minute mindfulness session for stress reduction, the science is clear. A modest time investment can significantly impact your well-being, reinforcing the principle that in the pursuit of health, every minute truly counts.

The Art of Time-Efficiency: Making the Most of Your 10 Minutes

In our contemporary, hustle-oriented culture, time is often depicted as a scarce resource. Phrases like "time is money" or "there are not enough hours in the day" encapsulate a common sentiment. Many people feel so overwhelmed by work commitments, family responsibilities, and social obligations that they deem themselves "too busy" to prioritize health. The irony, however, is that neglecting one's well-being often results in diminished productivity, creating a vicious cycle.

The 1% Investment

The beauty of dedicating just 10 minutes a day to activities like grounding, morning sunshine absorption, or deep breathing is that it amounts to a mere 1% of your day. When put into perspective, it's hard to justify not making that small investment. Ten minutes can pass by unnoticed while scrolling through social media, watching TV, or even waiting for your morning coffee to brew. The difference lies in how you choose to invest that time.

The Compound Effect

Just like compound interest in finance, where small, regular contributions can grow into a significant sum over time, the "compound effect" of daily 10-minute health investments can lead to remarkable long-term benefits. You're not just investing time; you're investing in a series of positive outcomes—better sleep quality, reduced stress levels, and overall well-being—that multiply over time. These outcomes, in turn, can lead to increased productivity and a higher quality of life, breaking the cycle of "too busy to be healthy."

Practicality Meets Impact

Ten minutes is a practically achievable goal that can seamlessly integrate into any part of your day. It can be a brief morning ritual before the day's chaos begins, a quick break from work to re-center, or a calming nighttime routine to wrap up your day. Despite its brevity, this 10-minute commitment is potent. Activities like grounding, absorbing morning sunshine, or engaging in deep breathing exercises are not merely placeholders in your schedule but scientifically-backed practices known for their immediate and long-term health benefits.

Rethinking Time Management

In conclusion, the concept of "I don't have time" is debunked when you consider the potency of a mere 10-minute investment in your well-being. By dedicating just 1% of your daily time to activities that improve your health, you're making a conscious choice to prioritize yourself. And when wellness becomes a priority, it's not just your health that benefits—you'll likely find that you have more energy, focus, and time to tackle the other 99% of your day.

The Democratization of Health: Embracing the Accessibility of 10-Minute Rituals

Breaking Down Barriers

When it comes to adopting a healthier lifestyle, a plethora of obstacles often stands in the way, some of which can be intimidating or even prohibitive. Gym memberships and specialized fitness equipment can be prohibitively expensive for many. Likewise, specialized diets often require a considerable investment of time and money into meal planning, grocery shopping, and preparation. Even if one musters the will to exercise, the challenge of fitting a comprehensive workout into an already-packed schedule can be discouraging. This is where the concept of a 10-minute health ritual shines as a beacon of accessibility.

No Excuses: Everyone Has 10 Minutes

The genius of a 10-minute routine lies in its universal applicability. Time—regardless of socioeconomic status, lifestyle, or existing commitments—is uniformly distributed. Each day gifts us 1,440 minutes, and the 10-minute commitment to your health requires less than 1% of that time. Whether you're waiting for your morning coffee to brew, taking a break during your lunch hour, or winding down before bed, there's always a window that can accommodate this modest yet transformative routine.

Simplifying Complexity

Specialized diets and elaborate workout plans often necessitate a steep learning curve. In contrast, the 10-minute health ritual is straightforward and simple to adopt. Whether it's grounding yourself in nature, soaking in the early morning sun, or practicing deep breathing, these activities do not require special skills, expensive equipment, or extensive prior knowledge. Essentially, they level the playing field, making better health attainable for everyone.

The Multiplying Effect of Accessibility

The accessibility of this 10-minute window also fosters consistency, which is the linchpin of any successful health regimen. The less cumbersome the routine, the more likely you are to stick with it. And once you establish this pattern, the benefits accumulate rapidly. What's more, as you begin to feel the positive impacts, the once-small commitment starts to feel less like a task and more like a treasured part of your day.

The Ultimate Equalizer

In a world that often seems to set the bar high for health and well-being, allocating just 10 minutes a day for yourself serves as the ultimate equalizer. It topples the barriers of cost, complexity, and time, rendering better health not just a possibility but an accessible reality for all. All you need to do is seize those 10 minutes and make them count.

The Dual Rewards: Immediate Gratification and Lasting Transformation Through 10-Minute Rituals

The Power of Instant Gratification

In a world conditioned to crave instant results, the immediate benefits of 10-minute rituals can be incredibly satisfying and motivating. Imagine starting your day by grounding yourself, perhaps walking barefoot on grass or soil. The sensory experience can instill a sense of calm and connectedness that you carry throughout the day. Or consider the uplifting impact of early morning sunshine; just a few minutes of natural light can enhance your mood, providing you with an almost instantaneous lift. Likewise, deep-breathing exercises can serve as a quick reset button for your stress levels, offering immediate relief from the ongoing pressures of the day.

Not Just a Quick Fix: The Compound Effect

While the immediate rewards are compelling, they are only the tip of the iceberg. What makes these 10-minute rituals revolutionary is their capacity to offer long-term benefits that compound over time. Consistent grounding practices, for example, have been shown to reduce inflammation, improve cardiovascular health, and enhance sleep quality. Similarly, consistent exposure to morning sunshine can help regulate your circadian rhythm, which in turn has far-reaching implications for your sleep, mood, and overall well-being. The benefits of deep breathing extend beyond momentary stress relief; studies have shown that regular practice can lead to lower blood pressure, improved mental clarity, and even a strengthened immune system.

From Quick Wins to Lifelong Rewards

Engaging in these 10-minute rituals creates a positive feedback loop. The immediate benefits serve as a potent form of encouragement, motivating you to incorporate these practices into your daily routine. As you continue, the long-term benefits begin to materialize, reinforcing your commitment to these practices. In essence, what starts as a simple 10-minute daily investment evolves into a life-altering habit, providing you with both immediate gratification and lasting transformation.

The Virtuous Cycle: Immediate Gains Fuel Long-term Commitment

It's easy to get discouraged when the benefits of a new health regimen take time to become apparent. However, the immediate rewards of these 10-minute practices offer an initial boost of encouragement, making it easier to stick to your commitment. As you continue to engage in these rituals, the long-term advantages compound, resulting in substantial and lasting improvements in both mental and physical well-being.

In Summary

The brilliance of 10-minute rituals lies in their dual benefit: they provide immediate rewards that serve as the catalyst for long-term transformation. This balance between quick wins and sustained benefits offers a holistic approach to health and well-being, making these simple rituals an essential part of a balanced, healthy life.

In short, the time to act is now. Ten minutes a day can change your life; all you need to do is start.

The Three Pillars: Grounding, Sunshine, Deep Breathing

Grounding: The Elemental Connection for Holistic Health

The Science Behind Grounding

Grounding, or "earthing" as it's also known, is more than a nostalgic return to our childhood days of running barefoot through the grass. It's an evidence-backed practice that capitalizes on the Earth's natural electrical charges. When we make direct contact with the Earth's surface—be it grass, soil, or sand—our bodies absorb these natural charges. The theory is that this helps to neutralize free radicals and combat inflammation, two underlying factors in a wide range of health conditions.

Grounding as a Radical Neutralizer

Free radicals are molecules with unpaired electrons, making them unstable and highly reactive. They can cause cellular damage and are often implicated in chronic conditions, from cardiovascular diseases to certain types of cancer. Grounding appears to act as a natural antioxidant, neutralizing these free radicals and thereby reducing oxidative stress. While the specific mechanisms are still the subject of ongoing research, early studies suggest that grounding may help reduce inflammation, a common marker for various health ailments.

The Benefits Extend Beyond Anti-Inflammation

Although reducing inflammation is one of the most commonly cited benefits of grounding, its potential advantages go far beyond that. Grounding has been linked to a variety of other health benefits:

1. **Improved Sleep Quality**: Studies have shown that grounding can improve sleep quality by normalizing the body's circadian rhythms. This could be particularly beneficial for those suffering from insomnia or irregular sleep patterns.

2. **Pain Reduction**: Preliminary research suggests that grounding may help in reducing chronic pain, possibly due to its anti-inflammatory effects.

3. **Enhanced Mental Well-being**: Some proponents of grounding assert that it helps in emotional regulation, reducing symptoms of anxiety and depression.

4. **Cardiovascular Health**: There's emerging evidence to suggest that grounding may also help regulate blood pressure and improve cardiovascular health.

A Simple, Yet Transformative Ritual

In a world where complex health regimens and expensive treatments often take center stage, grounding stands out for its simplicity. All it requires is direct contact with the Earth, no special equipment or gym membership needed. Whether it's a brief walk in your garden or standing on a sandy beach, grounding is a straightforward yet effective ritual that anyone can incorporate into their daily life.

In Summary

Grounding offers a range of health benefits that extend from the cellular level to your overall sense of well-being. By dedicating just a few minutes a day to this ancient practice, you can tap into the Earth's natural healing power, offering your body a foundation of wellness that can improve both your mental and physical health.

Early Morning Sunshine: Nature's Elixir for Holistic Health

The Clock-Setting Power of Morning Sunshine

The act of stepping into the early morning sunlight does much more than simply brighten your day—it actually sets your internal biological clock, also known as your circadian rhythm. This natural timekeeper regulates a variety of bodily functions, from your sleep-wake cycle to hormone release and metabolism. Morning sunlight sends signals to the brain to wake up and get active, helping to reset this internal clock and keep your biological processes in tune with the day.

The Vitamin D Factor

Beyond regulating circadian rhythms, early morning sunshine serves as an effective, natural source of Vitamin D—often referred to as the "sunshine vitamin." When ultraviolet rays from the sun interact with our skin, they trigger the synthesis of Vitamin D, a vital nutrient for several physiological functions:

1. **Bone Health**: Vitamin D plays a critical role in calcium absorption, essential for maintaining healthy bones and teeth. A deficiency in Vitamin D can lead to brittle bone conditions like osteoporosis.

2. **Immune Function**: It supports the immune system, helping your body fight off pathogens and reducing the risk of chronic diseases.

3. **Mental Well-being**: There is emerging research indicating that adequate levels of Vitamin D can help mitigate symptoms of depression and anxiety, enhancing your overall mood.

Metabolic Benefits

The sun's morning rays can also impact your metabolic rate. By helping to regulate your body's internal clock, morning sunshine indirectly influences metabolic processes such as digestion and calorie burning. This can be particularly beneficial for individuals focusing on weight management or metabolic health.

More Than Just Physical Benefits

In addition to the physical benefits, early morning sunshine can also enhance mental well-being. Exposure to natural light has been shown to boost mood, increase alertness, and improve mental performance. The psychological effects of basking in the morning sun should not be underestimated; they contribute to an overall sense of wellness that goes beyond the physical.

The Accessibility of Morning Sunshine

One of the beautiful aspects of incorporating early morning sunshine into your routine is its accessibility. Unlike many health interventions that require specialized equipment or facilities, all you need to harness the power of morning sunlight is to step outside. Whether it's enjoying a cup of coffee on your porch or taking a quick walk around the block, you have the opportunity to tap into this natural resource every day.

In Summary

Early morning sunshine offers a wealth of benefits that impact both your physical and mental health. From setting your internal clock and boosting Vitamin D production to enhancing metabolic and mental well-being, the advantages of morning light exposure are both significant and accessible. Just a few minutes basking in the morning sun can set a positive tone for the rest of your day, providing a holistic approach to health and wellness.

Deep Breathing: The 10-Minute Roadmap to a Calmer, More Focused You

More Than Relaxation: The Science of Deep Breathing

Deep breathing goes beyond the cliché of "taking a deep breath to relax." Scientifically, it impacts your autonomic nervous system, shifting the balance from its fight-or-flight response to its rest-and-digest mode. This is a particularly significant change because our modern lives are filled with stressors that keep us in a near-constant state of fight-or-flight, which is detrimental to both our mental and physical health.

Techniques That Transform: Diaphragmatic Breathing and the 4-7-8 Method

There are several deep-breathing techniques designed to help you harness these physiological benefits:

1. **Diaphragmatic Breathing**: Also known as "belly breathing," this technique focuses on engaging the diaphragm, allowing you to take deep and more efficient breaths. It helps you breathe in a way that maximizes the amount of oxygen that goes into your bloodstream, potentially increasing energy levels and reducing feelings of stress and anxiety.

2. **The 4-7-8 Method**: This technique involves breathing in through the nose for 4 seconds, holding the breath for 7 seconds, and then exhaling through the mouth for 8 seconds. This pattern aims to reduce anxiety, help people fall asleep faster, and manage cravings.

Immediate Hormonal Impact: Stress Hormones and Mental Clarity

Deep breathing has a tangible impact on your hormonal balance. Techniques like diaphragmatic breathing and the 4-7-8 method have been shown to reduce the levels of stress hormones like cortisol. A decrease in cortisol levels has a cascade of beneficial effects on the body, including reduced inflammation, lower blood pressure, and enhanced cognitive function.

10 Minutes to Regulation: The Nervous System Benefits

Incorporating just a 10-minute deep breathing session into your daily routine can bring immediate benefits, particularly in regulating your nervous system. A brief but focused period of deep breathing can quickly reduce your heart rate, lower blood pressure, and create a sense of calm. This regulatory effect on the nervous system provides immediate relief from stress, enhances your ability to focus, and can even improve your mood.

Mental Gains: Focus and Emotional Balance

While the physiological benefits of deep breathing are impressive, perhaps equally compelling are the cognitive and emotional gains. The practice has been shown to improve attention and focus, as it helps quiet the "noise" in your mind and makes it easier to concentrate. Furthermore, emotional regulation becomes easier, as deep breathing can help you maintain a balanced emotional state, making you less reactive to external stressors.

The Long-Term Magic: Sustained Benefits Over Time

The immediate benefits of deep breathing are substantial, but the true magic lies in its cumulative effect when practiced over time. Regular deep breathing can contribute to long-term emotional well-being, better stress management, and even a stronger immune system.

In Summary

Deep breathing stands as a powerful yet simple tool in your wellness toolkit. Its impact on the nervous system and hormonal balance delivers immediate benefits in stress reduction and improved focus. Moreover, when practiced consistently over time, it contributes to long-term health gains that can transform your quality of life. All it takes is a small, 10-minute daily commitment to reap these abundant rewards.

The Synergy of the Three Pillars: Amplifying Your Well-being Through Grounding, Early Morning Sunshine, and Deep Breathing

The Power of Unity: Beyond Individual Benefits

While grounding roots you to the Earth, early morning sunshine aligns your internal body clock, and deep breathing helps manage stress, each pillar's power amplifies when integrated into a single, unified routine. This is the concept of synergy, where the collective impact of these practices is greater than the sum of their individual benefits.

Natural Bio-rhythms: The Underpinning of Health

Grounding serves as the foundation of this synergetic model. By connecting directly to the Earth's natural electrical frequencies, you're not just grounding yourself in the literal sense; you're also reinforcing your body's natural bio-rhythms. This creates a baseline for physiological balance, from which other wellness activities can amplify their effects.

The Aligning Force: Early Morning Sunshine

Enter early morning sunshine, which takes this grounded state and elevates it by aligning your internal clock. Your circadian rhythm dictates various physiological processes—from your sleep-wake cycle to hormone secretion. When you expose yourself to natural light in the morning, you're giving your body the cue it needs to kickstart these processes in a way that's aligned with your natural rhythms. This can result in better sleep, a more effective metabolism, and an overall boost in your mood.

Deep Breathing: The Tying Knot

Deep breathing acts like the glue that binds these practices together. After grounding connects you to the Earth and early morning sunshine aligns your internal rhythms, deep breathing helps your body make the most of this aligned and balanced state. By practicing deep breathing techniques, you further reduce stress, improve focus, and enable your body to function at its best.

The Synergistic Outcome: Exponential Health Benefits

When you incorporate all three pillars—Grounding, Early Morning Sunshine, and Deep Breathing—into a daily 10-minute routine, you tap into a synergy that significantly amplifies your overall well-being. This means that not only do you enjoy the individual benefits of each pillar, but you also unlock a compounded effect that could include heightened mental clarity, stronger immune function, improved sleep quality, and a more stable emotional state.

Achieving Balance: Physical and Mental Symbiosis

What makes this synergy so potent is that it addresses both physical and mental well-being. Grounding and early morning sunshine largely target physical health, affecting everything from inflammation to vitamin D levels, while deep breathing focuses on mental wellness, reducing stress and improving focus. When combined, these practices offer a holistic approach to health that feels almost like a well-kept secret for achieving both physical and mental balance.

In Summary

Incorporating the synergy of Grounding, Early Morning Sunshine, and Deep Breathing into your daily routine isn't just another wellness fad; it's a science-backed strategy for achieving optimal health. By harnessing the synergistic effects of these three pillars, you significantly amplify the benefits, paving the way for a healthier, happier life.

Incorporating these three pillars—Grounding, Early Morning Sunshine, and Deep Breathing—into your daily life is not a Herculean task requiring monumental effort. It's as simple as dedicating 10 minutes a day to your well-being. By doing so, you tap into a holistic approach to health that covers both the physical and mental aspects of wellness.

What to Expect in This Book

This book is designed as a comprehensive guide to help you unlock a healthier, more vibrant version of yourself in just 10 minutes a day. Below is a brief summary of each chapter and what you can expect to learn:

Chapter 1: What is Grounding?

In this opening chapter, we introduce you to the concept of grounding, its historical roots, and the scientific evidence that backs its benefits for overall well-being.

Chapter 2: The Magic of Early Morning Sunshine

Here, we delve into the wonders of early morning sun exposure. Learn about the significance of Vitamin D and how the timing of your sun exposure can dramatically affect your health.

CHAPTER 3: THE SCIENCE OF DEEP BREATHING
We explore various deep breathing techniques, explaining how they work and why they're so effective for reducing stress and improving mental clarity.

CHAPTER 4: GROUNDING AND YOUR HEALTH
This chapter digs deeper into the specific health benefits of grounding, such as improved sleep quality and the reduction of chronic pain.

CHAPTER 5: EARLY MORNING SUNSHINE FOR WELLBEING
Discover how capturing those early morning rays can improve your mood, enhance your skin health, and contribute to your overall sense of well-being.

CHAPTER 6: DEEP BREATHING AND MINDFULNESS
We delve into the synergies between deep breathing and mindfulness, showing how they can reduce anxiety and stress while enhancing cognitive function.

CHAPTER 7: DESIGNING YOUR 10-MINUTE MORNING RITUAL
Learn how to create your personalized 10-minute morning ritual, incorporating all three pillars for maximum impact.

CHAPTER 8: THE 30-DAY CHALLENGE
Get a week-by week guide for a 30-day challenge aimed at helping you make these practices a part of your daily routine.

CHAPTER 9: OVERCOMING COMMON OBSTACLES
We address frequent hurdles like adverse weather conditions and busy schedules, offering practical solutions for staying committed to your health journey.

CHAPTER 10: ADVANCED TIPS AND HACKS
Learn about additional tools and locations that can enhance your 10-minute rituals, like grounding footwear and the best spots for absorbing early morning sunshine.

CONCLUSION: YOUR JOURNEY TO 10 X HEALTH
We wrap up by summarizing what you've learned and encouraging you to continue this transformative journey toward improved health and well-being.

By the end of this book, you'll not only be well-versed in the science behind each pillar but also equipped with the tools and tips to integrate them seamlessly into your daily life.

YOUR INVITATION

We've laid out the science, shared the testimonials, and provided you with step-by-step guides. Now, it's your turn to take action. We invite you to join our 30-day challenge—a month-long commitment to unlocking a healthier, happier you.

Making change isn't always easy, but it's usually simpler than we think. This 30-day challenge will give you the structure and support you need to make these three pillars—Grounding, Early Morning Sunshine, and Deep Breathing—a permanent fixture in your daily life. Commit to just 10 minutes a day for the next month, and witness firsthand the transformative power of these simple yet effective practices.

So are you in? Will you commit to making a change? Remember, the journey of a thousand miles begins with a single step—or in this case, just 10 minutes a day. Make that commitment now, and let's embark on this journey together towards exponential health and lifelong well-being.

CHAPTER 1: WHAT IS GROUNDING?

Unlocking the Earth's Power: An In-Depth Exploration of Grounding for Modern Wellness

Welcome to the fascinating world of grounding—a term that has been buzzing in health and wellness circles for good reason. Grounding, also commonly known as "earthing," represents more than just a modern trend; it's a return to our roots, quite literally. As society becomes increasingly disconnected from the natural world, caught up in the whirlwind of technology and hectic schedules, grounding offers us a way to reconnect with the Earth and, in the process, restore balance to our overtaxed bodies and minds.

The surge in interest in grounding is not by accident. It aligns with a growing body of scientific research that emphasizes the importance of our relationship with the Earth for optimal health. Whether you've stumbled upon the term in a wellness blog, heard it mentioned in a yoga class, or found it while searching for natural ways to improve your well-being, grounding has attracted attention for its simple yet profound potential to positively impact various aspects of our health.

This chapter aims to delve deep into what grounding really is, its historical context, and the scientific evidence that surrounds it. Consider this your comprehensive guide to understanding this age-old practice that has modern-day relevance. So let's dig in, shall we?

DEFINITION AND HISTORY

GROUNDING: THE SCIENCE AND SIMPLICITY OF EARTH CONNECTION FOR ENHANCED WELL-BEING

A SIMPLE PRACTICE WITH COMPLEX INTERACTIONS

At its core, grounding, or "earthing," is a straightforward practice: physically connecting your body to the Earth. This usually involves making direct contact with natural surfaces like soil, grass, or water, or even utilizing specially-designed grounding equipment. The primary aim is to channel the Earth's natural electrical charge into your body, fostering a range of physiological benefits. While the concept might sound incredibly basic, it serves as a gateway to a myriad of complex interactions between your body and the Earth—interactions that researchers are only just beginning to delve into.

THE TRANSFER OF EARTH'S NATURAL ENERGIES

The Earth is an electrical entity, teeming with natural currents and charges. When you ground yourself, you're essentially becoming a part of this electrical network, absorbing some of the Earth's energy. The process is believed to foster a range of physiological changes, from reduced inflammation to improved sleep quality. These are benefits that, although intuitive, are only now being substantiated through scientific research.

A DUAL NOMENCLATURE: GROUNDING VS. EARTHING

The terms "grounding" and "earthing" are often used interchangeably, but each brings a slightly different nuance to the practice. While grounding suggests the act of establishing a connection, earthing emphasizes a return to nature, a reconnection with the Earth's inherent energies. Both aim to describe a practice that serves as an interface between your body and the Earth, but "earthing" particularly stresses the origin and authenticity of this age-old practice.

Beyond the Obvious: Intricate Bodily Responses

Though it might seem like a simple act, grounding triggers an intricate set of physiological responses. Researchers are now exploring these with increasing interest, seeking to understand how the Earth's natural electrical charges interact with the human body. Whether these charges neutralize free radicals, reduce inflammation, or offer some other as-yet-unknown benefit, it's clear that the relationship between the Earth and human physiology is more complex than it may initially appear.

Multiple Avenues for Grounding

The beauty of grounding lies in its accessibility. Whether it's walking barefoot on a sandy beach, lounging on a grassy field, or even using specialized grounding mats or sheets, there are multiple ways to engage in this practice. Each offers the same core benefit: a chance to reconnect with the Earth's natural energies and potentially enhance your well-being.

Grounding as a Holistic Endeavor

The ultimate goal of grounding is holistic well-being. It's not just about the physical benefits, but also the subtle, yet profound, ways in which this practice can enhance your emotional and spiritual well-being. Reconnecting with the Earth can serve as a reminder of our intrinsic relationship with the natural world, a relationship that modern life often disrupts but which grounding seeks to restore.

Conclusion

Grounding is much more than a modern wellness trend; it's a primal practice that connects us to the Earth in a physically meaningful way. Its simplicity masks a complex interaction between our bodies and the Earth, an interaction that researchers are keenly exploring. Whether through walking barefoot, lying on the grass, or using dedicated equipment, grounding offers a simple yet potentially transformative avenue for enhancing both physical and emotional well-being.

Tracing the Roots and Resurgence of Grounding: A Journey from Ancient Wisdom to Modern Science

From Time Immemorial: Grounding in Ancient Cultures

The practice of grounding is far from a contemporary fad; it has historical roots deeply embedded in cultures worldwide. Indigenous communities across the globe, from Native Americans in the Americas to practitioners of ancient Ayurveda in India, have long recognized the Earth's therapeutic powers. Whether through specific earthing rituals or simply spending time in nature, the concept of grounding has served as a common thread that binds diverse civilizations over millennia.

The Neglect of a Vital Practice

Despite its ancient origins, grounding has been increasingly relegated to the margins of modern life. The onset of industrialization brought myriad conveniences that have indirectly severed our primal connection to the Earth. Rubber-soled shoes and predominantly indoor lifestyles, for example, have minimized our direct contact with natural surfaces. This modern disconnection has not only shifted cultural practices but has also sparked concerns among healthcare professionals about the potential health consequences.

A Scientific Wake-Up Call

Recognizing the implications of this detachment, the scientific community has increasingly turned its attention toward the benefits of re-establishing our link with the Earth. Various studies have been launched to explore grounding's physiological effects, from its potential to reduce inflammation to its role in enhancing sleep quality. These efforts have been significantly bolstered by advances in technology, which permit more precise measurement and understanding of how Earth's natural electrical charges interact with the human body.

The Confluence of Tradition and Technology

Today, we're witnessing a resurgence in the practice of grounding that marries ancient wisdom with modern scientific scrutiny. As a result, grounding is reclaiming its rightful place not just in popular health discourse but also in scientific research. This renaissance is supported by an increasingly sophisticated array of technologies that allow for more nuanced study, from bioelectrical impedance analysis to advanced oxidative stress markers.

Conclusion

Grounding's journey from an intuitive, traditional practice to a subject of rigorous scientific investigation is a compelling testament to its enduring relevance. As the practice gains renewed attention and credibility, it serves as a powerful reminder of the fundamental relationship between humans and the Earth—a relationship that, thanks in part to modern science, we are learning to appreciate and understand more deeply than ever before.

In summary, what was once an intuitive practice has evolved into a subject of rigorous scientific exploration, bringing grounding back into the limelight as both an ancient wisdom and a modern wellness practice.

Scientific Evidence

The Electrical Symphony of Grounding: Bridging Physics, Biology, and Wellness

The Human Body: A Marvel of Electrical Engineering

Our bodies are intricate webs of electrical activity. Each cell operates like a tiny electrical unit, contributing to the complex signaling networks that govern everything from our heartbeats to our synaptic firing. Neurons send electrical impulses that guide our movements, thoughts, and sensations. Even at the biochemical level, processes such as cellular respiration are mediated by flows of electrons. In essence, we are walking, talking bundles of electrical energy.

Earth: The Grand Conductor

The Earth isn't just a mass of land and water; it's a dynamic electrical entity. It possesses its own electromagnetic field, which acts like a colossal circuit board conducting energy. This planetary field is continuously interacting with all living beings and systems on its surface, although the subtleties of this interaction are still a subject of ongoing research.

An Electric Union: Grounding and Electromagnetic Harmony

When we engage in grounding practices, like walking barefoot on soil or lying on the grass, we enter into an electrical partnership with the Earth. The skin, our body's largest organ, acts as a conductive interface. As we make direct contact with Earth, we create a pathway for the planet's natural electric charge to enter our bodies. This electrical influx is not just a fleeting phenomenon but has the potential to interact with our cellular machinery.

Regulatory Rhythms: Grounding's Impact on Internal Systems

The idea that this electrical interaction has physiological benefits is more than folklore; it's gaining traction in the scientific community. Researchers hypothesize that the Earth's electrical energy can help regulate various internal systems. For example, some studies suggest that grounding can neutralize free radicals—unstable molecules that contribute to inflammation and aging. Others indicate that grounding may help regulate circadian rhythms, thereby improving sleep quality. While many of these claims are still under scrutiny, the central idea remains: that grounding serves as a natural modulator for our body's electrical signaling and various physiological processes.

Conclusion

In grounding, we find an awe-inspiring intersection between physics and biology, between the Earth's raw electrical power and our own bioelectrical complexity. The exchange of energy that occurs during grounding seems to offer a way to recalibrate our internal systems, to bring them back into a state of equilibrium. As scientific inquiry deepens, we can only expect to uncover more about this fascinating dialogue between Earth and body, revealing new layers of understanding about our interconnectedness with the natural world.

The Empirical Landscape of Grounding: From Preliminary Findings to Promising Frontiers

The Shift from Theoretical to Empirical

For many years, grounding has been seen mostly through the lens of theoretical speculation or cultural practices. However, the tides are turning. Scientific studies have emerged, giving empirical heft to the theoretical underpinnings of grounding. While much of this research is still in its infancy, these empirical studies signal the beginning of a more rigorous understanding of how grounding affects health.

The Spectrum of Health Benefits

One of the most compelling aspects of grounding research is the range of health benefits it appears to offer. Early studies have pointed to noticeable improvements in sleep quality among participants who engaged in grounding. Other research has looked into grounding's ability to reduce inflammation—a critical factor in many chronic diseases. Moreover, grounding has shown promise in aiding stress management, helping to alleviate anxiety and improving mental well-being.

Diverse Research Methodologies

Research into grounding employs a variety of methodologies, from controlled clinical trials to observational case studies. For example, some studies use specialized grounding mats or sheets to ensure that participants are indeed being grounded. Others employ physiological markers such as cortisol levels, heart rate variability, or inflammatory biomarkers to quantify the effects. This diversity of approaches contributes to a richer, albeit still complex, understanding of grounding's impact.

Anecdotal Evidence and Case Studies

In addition to controlled scientific studies, a wealth of anecdotal evidence and case studies corroborate the potential benefits of grounding. Individuals who have incorporated grounding into their daily lives report significant improvements in well-being, from better sleep and less pain to improved mental clarity. While anecdotal accounts don't possess the scientific rigor of peer-reviewed studies, they provide valuable supplementary information that guides further research.

Caveats and Future Directions

It's important to note that while the existing body of research is promising, the majority of these studies are still preliminary. As of now, most have small sample sizes, short durations, or other limitations that warrant cautious interpretation. Yet, they pave the way for more comprehensive, large-scale studies that could definitively establish the efficacy of grounding as a health intervention.

Conclusion

The empirical study of grounding has crossed the threshold from theoretical musings to a field with a growing repository of scientific evidence. This shift represents a promising frontier, teasing a future where grounding might not just be an alternative practice but a scientifically endorsed method for enhancing well-being. As researchers continue to probe, the mysteries of how something as simple as connecting to the Earth can have such profound health benefits are waiting to be unlocked.

Skepticism and Criticisms in Grounding Research: A Necessary Counterpoint to Popular Enthusiasm

The Boom of Popularity and the Rise of Skepticism

As grounding garners more attention, particularly in health and wellness circles, skepticism naturally follows. Critics argue that the popularization of grounding has led to a premature acceptance of its efficacy without the robust scientific backing that a health practice should ideally have. This skepticism serves as a counterpoint, forcing proponents to question and validate their claims, thereby strengthening the science of grounding in the long run.

The Gap in Large-Scale, Long-Term Studies

One of the most common criticisms aimed at grounding research is the absence of large-scale, long-term studies. Most research conducted so far consists of small sample sizes and shorter durations, which limits the generalizability of the findings. Critics argue that without such comprehensive studies, it is difficult to fully endorse grounding as an effective health practice.

The Placebo Effect Debate

Another major point of contention is the role of the placebo effect. Skeptics often suggest that the reported benefits of grounding may be due to the psychological impact of believing in its effectiveness, rather than any physiological changes induced by the practice itself. While the placebo effect is a valid consideration in any health intervention, it also offers an avenue for further research to distinguish between perceived and actual benefits.

The Need for Scientific Rigor

The criticisms make it clear that grounding research must be approached with scientific rigor. This involves not just developing more rigorous methodologies but also diversifying study designs to address criticisms head-on. For example, future research could employ double-blind controlled trials to eliminate any placebo effects and provide more reliable data.

Early Stages and Promising Future

Despite the criticisms, it's crucial to remember that the field of grounding research is still relatively young. The ongoing scientific inquiry into this practice holds great promise for teasing apart anecdotal claims from empirical evidence. The scrutiny from skeptics could actually serve as a catalyst, pushing the field toward more robust, evidence-based conclusions.

Conclusion

Skepticism and criticisms are not roadblocks but rather critical components of any evolving field of study. They introduce a level of scrutiny that challenges researchers to improve their methodologies and refine their claims. While grounding research has its fair share of detractors, their skepticism serves a vital function: to ensure that the practice stands up to the highest standards of scientific evidence before it is fully integrated into mainstream health and wellness strategies.

In summary, grounding stands on a growing body of scientific research, with continued exploration likely to provide deeper insights into its effects on our well-being.

Conclusion

By now, you should have a well-rounded understanding of what grounding is—an ancient practice that involves making direct contact with the Earth to harness its natural electrical energy. You've seen how this seemingly simple act is rooted in both historical traditions and modern scientific inquiry. We've explored the electrical nature of our own bodies, the Earth's electromagnetic field, and how the two interact in ways that could profoundly affect our health. While some skepticism exists, a growing body of empirical studies and anecdotal evidence points toward grounding's potential benefits, setting the stage for more rigorous scientific scrutiny in the future.

As we move into the next chapter, we'll shift from theory to application. Armed with this foundational knowledge, you're well-prepared to explore the various ways grounding can manifest its benefits in your life, from improved sleep quality to reduced chronic pain. The subsequent chapters will serve as your guide to integrating grounding into your daily routine and experiencing firsthand the transformative power of connecting with the Earth.

Your journey to a healthier life, rooted in both science and nature, is just beginning.

CHAPTER 2: THE MAGIC OF EARLY MORNING SUNSHINE

The Transformative Power of Early Morning Sunshine—More Than Just a Light Source

The Sun: A Luminous Catalyst for Well-Being—Beyond Light to the Essence of Life

It's easy to underestimate the sun's influence by viewing it solely as a provider of light and warmth. Yet, this celestial orb plays a far more profound and multifaceted role in human well-being. It doesn't just illuminate our world; it vitalizes it, becoming a life source that deeply affects both our physical and mental states.

To truly appreciate the sun's influence, it's important to consider the intricate web of biological and biochemical processes it regulates. Plants, the foundation of all terrestrial life, rely on the sun for photosynthesis, converting solar energy into chemical energy and producing oxygen as a byproduct. This oxygen not only sustains our respiratory needs but also sets the stage for complex ecosystems to thrive, thereby establishing the sun as a cornerstone of life on Earth.

But the sun's influence goes beyond the environmental scale to deeply personal levels. Solar rays stimulate intricate biochemical reactions within the human body, a delicate dance of processes that can profoundly impact our health and well-being. For instance, exposure to ultraviolet (UV) rays triggers the synthesis of Vitamin D, a hormone crucial for bone health, immune function, and mental well-being. The sun also plays a vital role in regulating circadian rhythms, our internal body clocks that manage sleep-wake cycles, hormone release, and even mood. By affecting the secretion of melatonin and serotonin, the sun can elevate our mood, reduce stress, and improve overall mental health.

In essence, the sun is not merely a bright ball of gas emitting light; it's a complex, life-sustaining system that deeply enriches our existence. Its rays act as catalysts, sparking a cascade of beneficial biochemical reactions that enhance our physical health, regulate biological rhythms, and uplift our psychological state. When we consider the sun in this expansive way, it transcends its role as a mere light source and takes its rightful place as a luminous catalyst for comprehensive well-being.

The Unique Allure of Early Morning Sunshine: A Balanced Symphony of Light for Holistic Well-Being

While it's true that the sun benefits us throughout the day, there's something almost magical about the first rays of morning sunshine. This exceptional window of time offers a unique blend of solar qualities that bring about a spectrum of health benefits, both physically and psychologically. It's as if nature has designed the early morning to be a sanctuary for our well-being.

The early morning sun emits a balanced spectrum of light that serves multiple purposes. For one, it provides the essential ultraviolet (UV) rays needed for Vitamin D synthesis. Vitamin D is indispensable for various bodily functions, including bone health and immune system regulation. Concurrently, the morning sun's softer, warm hues contribute positively to our mental state and circadian rhythm. This balanced composition of light frequencies essentially "tunes" our internal biological clocks, aligning them with the natural rhythms of the day. The outcome is a cascade of benefits including better sleep quality, more consistent energy levels, and an improved sense of well-being.

Beyond its biochemical impact, early morning sunshine offers another compelling advantage: gentleness. Unlike the harsh midday sun, which can increase the risk of sunburn and skin damage, the early morning sun is typically softer on the skin. This means you can soak up its benefits with less concern about the potential adverse effects, making it an optimal time for those who are sensitive to sunlight or are cautious about skin health.

This balance of potency and gentleness creates a magical window, where the sun offers a comprehensive set of benefits that transcend mere illumination. It becomes a holistic tool for improving physical health, regulating emotional states, and even fine-tuning our internal body clocks. As we explore the rest of this chapter, you'll gain deeper insights into how this unique period can be harnessed for maximal benefits. Whether you're new to the practice of basking in the morning sun or are looking to optimize an existing routine, understanding the unique allure of early morning sunshine equips you with the knowledge to enhance your overall well-being in a harmonious and natural way.

VITAMIN D AND BEYOND: UNVEILING THE MULTIFACETED BENEFITS OF SUN EXPOSURE

THE SUNSHINE VITAMIN: A CORNERSTONE OF HEALTH

When your skin is exposed to the sun, specifically the ultraviolet B (UVB) rays, it triggers a biological process that converts cholesterol in your skin cells into Vitamin D3. This form of Vitamin D then undergoes a series of transformations in the liver and kidneys to become the active hormone known for its vital health benefits.

STRENGTHENING THE FRAMEWORK OF YOUR HEALTH: THE CRUCIAL ROLE OF VITAMIN D IN BONE INTEGRITY

Vitamin D is not just another nutrient; it's a cornerstone in the architecture of your physical well-being, particularly when it comes to bone health. While it might be most famously known for helping to fend off colds or elevate your mood, its role in maintaining strong bones cannot be overstated.

When ultraviolet B (UVB) rays from the sun interact with your skin, they kickstart a biological process that transforms cholesterol in skin cells into Vitamin D3. This D3 form is then converted into its active form in the liver and kidneys, where it becomes a hormone-like substance that circulates throughout the body. One of its primary destinations is the gut, where it facilitates the absorption of calcium—a mineral that is central to bone formation, density, and strength.

Calcium alone cannot effectively make its way into your bones without adequate levels of Vitamin D. Think of Vitamin D as the gatekeeper that allows calcium to be absorbed into the bloodstream. From there, calcium integrates into your bones, fortifying them and increasing their density. This interplay between Vitamin D and calcium is critical in preventing conditions that result from weak or brittle bones, such as osteoporosis and rickets.

Osteoporosis is a condition where the bones become porous and fragile, significantly increasing the risk of fractures. Rickets, although less common, is another severe bone condition that primarily affects children and results in weak, soft, and misshapen bones. Both of these conditions can have life-altering consequences, affecting mobility and quality of life.

Given the rise in indoor lifestyles and increased use of sunscreen, Vitamin D deficiencies are becoming more common. When you consider the severe impact a deficiency can have on bone health, the importance of sufficient sun exposure or Vitamin D supplementation becomes glaringly apparent.

In summary, Vitamin D serves as a linchpin in the complex system that maintains bone health. By ensuring you have adequate levels of this crucial vitamin, you're not just catching some rays; you're laying the foundation for a stronger, more resilient skeletal structure that will serve you well throughout your life.

THE IMMUNOLOGICAL SYMPHONY: HOW VITAMIN D FINE-TUNES YOUR BODY'S DEFENSE MECHANISMS

Vitamin D's role in the body goes far beyond supporting bone health; it's an essential player in the orchestration of your immune system. Emerging research has started to unravel the nuanced ways in which Vitamin D acts as an immunomodulator—a substance that can both amplify and temper the body's immune response, depending on what is needed.

When harmful pathogens, like bacteria and viruses, invade your body, specialized white blood cells called monocytes and macrophages are among the first responders. These cells have the critical job of identifying, attacking, and eliminating invaders. Vitamin D enhances the pathogen-fighting capabilities of these cells, essentially "arming" them with the tools they need to effectively neutralize threats. This makes the presence of Vitamin D crucial in the body's frontline defense against infectious diseases.

However, Vitamin D's influence on the immune system isn't solely about boosting its offensive capabilities; it's also about knowing when to pull back to prevent collateral damage. Inflammation is a natural response to infection or injury, but excessive inflammation can lead to tissue damage and various chronic diseases. Vitamin D has been shown to play a role in modulating this inflammatory response. It does so by inhibiting the release of pro-inflammatory cytokines, which are signaling molecules that promote inflammation. This not only helps to control the immune response but also minimizes the risk of it becoming overzealous and turning against the body's own tissues.

In light of this, a deficiency in Vitamin D can be particularly problematic. It could mean a weaker initial defense against pathogens and a higher likelihood of an imbalanced inflammatory response, which could lead to complications in the healing process or even chronic conditions.

The recognition of Vitamin D's influence on immune function expands our understanding of its importance far beyond its traditional roles. It's not just a vitamin; it's a multifunctional agent that fine-tunes our immune responses, ensuring they are balanced and effective. Therefore, adequate levels of Vitamin D—achieved either through sufficient sun exposure or supplementation—are not just advisable but critical for maintaining a well-functioning immune system.

The Neurochemical Ballet: How Vitamin D Influences Mood and Emotional Well-Being

Often touted for its critical role in bone health and immune function, Vitamin D is a lesser-known but increasingly recognized influencer in the realm of mental health. Its impact on mood stabilization makes it a compelling subject of study for neuroscientists and psychologists alike. While it may not replace conventional treatments for mood disorders, understanding Vitamin D's role could offer additional avenues for enhancing emotional well-being.

Vitamin D receptors are not just limited to bones or the immune system; they are also extensively distributed throughout the brain, including in regions responsible for regulating mood, such as the hippocampus and hypothalamus. This widespread presence is a strong indicator of Vitamin D's potential significance in mental health.

Research is gradually unveiling how adequate levels of Vitamin D can stabilize mood and potentially act as a protective factor against mood disorders like depression and anxiety. Several studies suggest that Vitamin D can influence the production and function of neurotransmitters like serotonin and dopamine, which are key chemicals involved in regulating mood, focus, and emotional well-being. A deficiency in Vitamin D has been correlated with lowered serotonin levels, which could result in symptoms of depression and anxiety.

Moreover, Vitamin D's anti-inflammatory properties might extend to the realm of mental health. Inflammation has been increasingly linked to various psychiatric conditions, including depression. Vitamin D's capacity to modulate inflammatory responses could, in theory, extend to neuroinflammation, potentially alleviating symptoms associated with mood imbalances.

It's crucial to note that while a deficiency in Vitamin D could contribute to mood swings or depressive states, supplementation alone may not be a complete solution for mental health issues, which are often complex and multi-causal. However, maintaining adequate levels of Vitamin D can be an important component in a multifaceted approach to mental health care.

In summary, Vitamin D plays an intriguing and complex role in mood regulation. Its influence on neurotransmitter activity, widespread presence in brain regions related to emotion, and its role in inflammation modulation all point towards its integral part in promoting emotional stability. Thus, ensuring sufficient levels of this vital nutrient—be it through sun exposure, diet, or supplementation—may offer a valuable strategy for improving emotional health and overall well-being.

Beyond Vitamin D: Delving into Additional Benefits

The sun's influence isn't limited to Vitamin D production; it has a broad range of other health-optimizing effects:

The Symbiotic Dance of Serotonin and Melatonin: How Sunlight Fine-Tunes Your Brain Chemistry

Sunlight, especially during the morning hours, does more than just brighten your surroundings; it also brightens your mood and optimizes your sleep cycle. This is largely due to the influence of sunlight on the production and regulation of two key hormones in your body—serotonin and melatonin. These hormones have a profound effect on your mental and physical state, serving functions that range from mood elevation to sleep quality.

The Sunshine Hormone: Serotonin's Role in Mood and Well-Being

Serotonin, often called the "happiness hormone," plays a pivotal role in regulating mood, appetite, and even social behavior. Exposure to natural sunlight in the morning stimulates the production of serotonin. This is because the sun's rays trigger specific cells in the retina, which then send signals to the brain to release this vital neurotransmitter. As a result, serotonin levels tend to rise, leading to enhanced mood, reduced anxiety, and a general sense of well-being. This makes morning sunlight a natural and effective mood enhancer that could potentially serve as a complementary treatment for mood disorders like depression and anxiety.

Nighttime's Maestro: Melatonin and the Quality of Sleep

On the flip side of the coin is melatonin, the hormone responsible for regulating sleep. Unlike serotonin, which is stimulated by the presence of light, melatonin is produced in darkness. However, the production and regulation of melatonin are profoundly affected by your exposure to natural light during the day. The reason is biological; your internal body clock, or circadian rhythm, uses natural light cues to set itself. When you expose yourself to sunlight during the day, especially in the morning, it helps your body understand when it should be awake and when it should prepare for sleep. This leads to better regulation of melatonin levels as darkness falls, making it easier for you to fall asleep and stay asleep through the night.

The interplay between serotonin and melatonin is a classic example of biological balance. Your body needs both in the right amounts at the right times to function optimally. Too little serotonin can lead to mood disorders, while an imbalance in melatonin can wreak havoc on your sleep. Therefore, exposure to morning sunlight serves as a natural modulator that helps maintain this delicate balance.

In essence, the sun's impact on serotonin and melatonin levels goes far beyond mere Vitamin D production. It acts as a natural bio-regulator, setting the tempo for your body's daily rhythms and cycles, thereby contributing to your overall mental and physical well-being.

The Sun as the Maestro of Your Internal Clock: How Morning Light Orchestrates Your Circadian Rhythm

Your body operates on an internal clock known as the circadian rhythm, a complex system of biochemical processes that governs everything from your sleep-wake cycles to hormone secretion and metabolism. This internal clock is not entirely self-sustained; it requires external cues, or "zeitgebers," to keep it in sync with the 24-hour day. The most powerful of these cues is natural light, especially morning sunlight.

The Morning Reset: Sunlight as the Sync Button

When you expose yourself to the morning sun, photoreceptors in your eyes capture the light and send signals to the suprachiasmatic nucleus (SCN) in the hypothalamus—the central clock of your brain. This exposure acts like a "sync" button for your internal clock, helping it align more closely with the natural day-night cycle. This is particularly significant in the morning, as this is when the light has a balanced spectrum that's highly effective for clock resetting. It serves as a natural "time-setter," telling your body that it's the start of a new day, and thus regulating a cascade of biological activities like hormone secretion, metabolism, and alertness levels.

Consistent Energy and Enhanced Performance

As your circadian rhythm gets calibrated by morning sunlight, one of the most noticeable effects is on your energy levels. Instead of experiencing energy slumps or spikes at irregular intervals, your body becomes better at distributing energy in a consistent manner throughout the day. This has implications not only for physical stamina but also for cognitive functions like attention, memory, and problem-solving skills. The better-aligned your circadian rhythm, the more efficient and productive you tend to be.

The Prelude to Quality Sleep

The benefits of morning sun exposure don't end as the sun sets; they extend into the night by enhancing the quality of your sleep. By setting your internal clock in the morning, you're effectively setting the stage for the rise in melatonin levels come evening. Melatonin is often called the "sleep hormone" because of its role in inducing and maintaining sleep. The more calibrated your internal clock is, the more effective the natural rise and fall of melatonin, allowing for better sleep quality and duration.

In summary, morning sun exposure plays an indispensable role in setting and maintaining your body's circadian rhythm, leading to a range of benefits that include more consistent energy levels, better cognitive performance, and enhanced sleep quality. So the next time you consider hitting the snooze button, remember that stepping outside to catch those first rays of morning light could make all the difference in how you feel, perform, and rest throughout the day.

Morning Sunlight and Your Skin: The Beauty Benefits of Moderation and Timing

While the sun has often been demonized for its potential to harm the skin through overexposure, it's crucial to remember that not all sun exposure is bad. In fact, moderate amounts, especially during the early morning, can be highly beneficial for your skin's health and appearance. The key lies in understanding the type of rays, their intensity, and the duration of exposure.

A Balanced Spectrum: The Gentle Morning Rays

Early morning sunlight is a unique blend of ultraviolet (UV) and visible rays. Unlike the harsher, more direct rays of midday, the morning sun offers a softer, more balanced spectrum. This means that you get enough UV radiation to kickstart various skin processes without the risk of immediate sunburn or long-term damage.

Natural Antibacterial Effects: The Acne-Fighting Power of the Sun

One of the most remarkable benefits of moderate sun exposure is its natural antibacterial effects. The sun's UV rays have been shown to kill bacteria, including the bacteria that can cause acne. While it's not a substitute for a comprehensive skincare routine, the sun's antibacterial properties can serve as a supplementary treatment for acne-prone skin. The morning sun, with its softer rays, allows for a safer antibacterial effect, enabling you to fight acne without the associated risks of sunburn or skin damage.

A Boost in Collagen Production: Towards Improved Complexion

Collagen is the primary protein in your skin, responsible for maintaining its structure and elasticity. Sunlight stimulates the production of vitamin D, which in turn can trigger collagen production. However, it's a double-edged sword: excessive UV radiation can break down collagen and accelerate aging. But here again, the morning sun comes to the rescue. The lower intensity of morning rays minimizes the risk of collagen breakdown, enabling the benefits without the drawbacks.

Precautions and Balance: The Need for Moderation

While the benefits are enticing, it's crucial to remember that moderation is key. Too much sun exposure can reverse these benefits and contribute to skin problems, including premature aging and an increased risk of skin cancer. Always use sun protection measures such as sunscreen or protective clothing when you expect to be in the sun for extended periods.

In conclusion, the softer rays of the morning sun offer a unique opportunity for skin care. From its natural antibacterial effects to its role in stimulating collagen production, moderate exposure during this magical morning window can be a potent ally in your skincare regimen. It's yet another way that the sun, often viewed as a mere source of light and heat, continues to reveal its complex and multi-faceted role in our well-being.

So as you can see, bathing in the morning sun does more than just make you feel good; it is a key component in a multifaceted approach to overall wellness. The benefits extend from bone health to emotional well-being, and from sleep quality to skin health, making it an indispensable part of a holistic health regimen.

How Timing Matters: Unlocking the Optimal Benefits of Sun Exposure

The Golden Hour: Nature's Perfect Timing for Optimal Health and Well-Being

The term "Golden Hour" has long been associated with photographers who chase this magical window for the perfect shot. But beyond the realm of aesthetics, the golden hour holds invaluable health benefits that are too significant to be ignored. It's a period that Mother Nature has beautifully crafted to deliver some of the most vital needs for our body while minimizing potential harm.

Sun Angle: A Harmonious Blend of UV Rays

During the golden hour, the sun is at a unique angle—low in the sky—that is highly favorable for human health. This positioning allows the sun's rays to filter through a thicker layer of Earth's atmosphere. This natural filtration system scatters the shorter, harmful blue and violet wavelengths of the spectrum, leaving behind the longer, more beneficial red and orange wavelengths. What we receive is a gentle, diffused light that's less likely to damage the skin.

The UV Balance: Safeguarding While Nourishing

One of the unique advantages of the golden hour is the UV ray composition. UVA rays, which are more abundant but less beneficial, are naturally filtered out more than UVB rays, which are essential for Vitamin D production. This gives us the best of both worlds: the rays that are most useful for our health, without the ones that are potentially damaging. It's like having a natural sunscreen that lets only the good rays through.

The Mood and Visual Ambiance: Beyond Physical Health

The warm, soft light during the golden hour is not just pleasing to the eyes but also beneficial for mental well-being. The red and orange hues have been associated with relaxation and calmness, potentially reducing stress and preparing the body and mind for the restful evening ahead or the active day that's just beginning.

The Quality of Light: A Healing Spectrum

What adds a touch of magic to the golden hour is the spectrum of light it offers. This spectrum is not just less harmful but also more effective in delivering health benefits. The longer wavelengths have been shown to be more efficient in supporting Vitamin D synthesis, setting the stage for a host of benefits, from improved bone health to enhanced mood regulation.

The Golden Hour Globally: A Universal Gift with Local Flavors

While the concept of the golden hour is universal, its timing and quality can vary depending on your geographic location, offering a unique blend that's perfectly suited for the local ecosystem. This adaptability makes the golden hour a universal yet personalized health gift from nature.

In conclusion, the golden hour is much more than a visual spectacle; it's a well-timed, well-filtered, and well-balanced window of opportunity for holistic well-being. By understanding its unique properties, you can harness this daily phenomenon to optimize your health, both mentally and physically.

Timing and Geography: Tailoring Your Sun Exposure Routine to Your Locale and Lifestyle

While the benefits of the golden hour are globally acknowledged, how you can best harness those advantages can greatly depend on your specific geographical location, the current season, and even daily weather conditions. It's like having a universally beneficial natural phenomenon that still demands a personalized approach to get the most out of it.

Latitude Variations: Equator Versus Higher Latitudes

Near the equator, the sun has a more vertical trajectory, making for a shorter golden hour but delivering more concentrated UVB rays. This can be ideal for quick bursts of sun exposure that are rich in the essential rays required for Vitamin D production. However, in higher latitudes, especially during winter, the sun takes a more slanted path across the sky, extending the duration of the golden hour but offering less intense UVB rays. While you'll still gain the benefits of this magical hour, you may need to spend a longer time outside to get the same amount of Vitamin D.

Seasonal Changes: The Sun's Seasonal Mood Swings

It's not just the location that impacts the quality of sun exposure; even the time of year plays a significant role. During the summer months, UVB rays are generally more abundant due to the sun's higher position in the sky. This makes Vitamin D production more efficient. In contrast, winter months offer a more extended but less Vitamin D-rich golden hour. Knowing this can help you adjust your outdoor activities to ensure you're getting the most benefit throughout the year.

Practical Tips: Localizing Your Sun Routine

1. **Weather and UV Index**: Always check the local weather and UV index forecasts before planning your sun exposure. High UV indices may mean you need less time in the sun to achieve the same benefits.
2. **Sun Timings**: Use mobile apps or traditional almanacs to find out the precise timings for sunrise and sunset in your area. This will help you pinpoint the golden hour for your specific location.
3. **Adjust for Seasons**: Consider the time of year when planning your sun exposure routine. You may need to adjust the duration based on the availability and intensity of UVB rays as the seasons change.

By understanding these variables, you can tailor your sun-exposure routine to maximize the benefits while minimizing the risks. It's like having a personalized solar prescription that adapts to your location, the time of year, and even the day's specific conditions.

Timing and Skin Type: Crafting a Sun Exposure Strategy Tailored to Your Unique Dermatological Needs

When it comes to soaking up the sun's rays, one size definitely doesn't fit all. The way your skin reacts to sunlight is influenced by a multitude of factors, including your skin type. Recognizing these nuances can help you create a sun exposure routine that is not just effective but also safe.

Duration of Exposure: The Skin Color Spectrum

Skin pigmentation plays a significant role in determining how quickly you can synthesize Vitamin D. Fair-skinned individuals, who have less melanin, might need just 10-15 minutes in the golden hour to achieve adequate levels of Vitamin D. On the other hand, those with darker skin tones, who have more melanin, may require up to an hour or more to absorb enough UVB rays for the same benefit. Melanin acts as a natural sunscreen; while it offers some protection against sunburn, it also slows down Vitamin D production.

Skin Health Precautions: Protecting Your Skin While You Benefit

1. **Sunscreen Usage**: Even though the golden hour offers softer rays, extended exposure to any kind of sunlight can be damaging. Sunscreen is crucial if you plan to be outdoors for long periods, especially outside the golden hour. Opt for broad-spectrum sunscreens that protect against both UVA and UVB rays.

2. **Medication Awareness**: Certain medications can make your skin more sensitive to sunlight, potentially causing burns or rashes even in the golden hour. If you're on any medications, consult with your healthcare provider about how they might interact with sun exposure.

3. **Patch Tests and Sensitivity**: Especially if you're new to a sun-exposure routine, consider doing a patch test to see how your skin reacts before diving in for longer periods.

4. **Regular Skin Checks**: Make it a habit to examine your skin regularly for any changes or irregularities. Early detection of issues like sunburn or sunspots can help you adjust your routine before they escalate into more serious conditions.

By being mindful of your skin type and any other personal variables, you can tailor your sun-exposure regimen to suit your individual needs. This personalized approach ensures that you are maximizing the benefits of the sun while taking prudent precautions to protect your skin.

In conclusion, timing is a crucial aspect that dictates the potential benefits you can reap from sun exposure. By paying attention to the golden hour, geographical location, and personal skin type, you can tailor a sun-exposure routine that maximizes benefits while minimizing risks.

The Transformative Power of Early Morning Sunshine and What Lies Ahead

As we've explored in this chapter, the sun offers far more than just a source of light—it's a multifaceted contributor to our overall well-being. From kickstarting our body's production of Vitamin D to its role in bone health, immune function, and mood regulation, the importance of sun exposure cannot be overstated. Beyond Vitamin D, the sun also positively impacts our serotonin and melatonin levels, helping to improve our circadian rhythms and sleep quality. It even bestows skin benefits like acne reduction and improved complexion.

However, as we've learned, it's not just about stepping outside at any time. Timing is of the essence. The golden hour provides a unique window where the quality of sunlight is at its best, balancing both safety and effectiveness. By also considering geographical and personal factors like latitude, season, and skin type, we can optimize this already beneficial interaction with our closest star.

So what's next? Armed with this knowledge, you're ready to integrate early morning sunshine into your daily routine in a meaningful way. As you look to improve your overall health and well-being, it's worth noting that sun exposure is just one piece of the puzzle. In the upcoming chapter, we'll delve into another elemental practice—deep breathing. Just as the sun invigorates us with its light, mastering the art of deep breathing can fill us with life-enhancing oxygen, a perfect complement to the benefits gleaned from early morning sunshine.

Stay tuned as we continue this journey towards a holistically healthier you.

CHAPTER 3: THE SCIENCE OF DEEP BREATHING

Unlocking the Transformative Power of Deep Breathing for Holistic Health

In Chapter 1, we delved into the fascinating world of grounding—exploring its historical roots and the scientific studies that support its potential benefits. Now, we're about to journey into another critical aspect of your well-being: the science of deep breathing.

If you think deep breathing is merely a relaxation technique you've skimmed over in a yoga class or stumbled upon in a stress management article, prepare to have your mind expanded. Deep breathing is more than just an antidote to stress; it's a powerful tool that can significantly improve both your physical and mental well-being.

This chapter will unravel the layers of this seemingly simple action—breathing. We'll explore how mastering the quality and pattern of your breath can not only equip you to handle stress and anxiety better but also optimize your body's overall functioning.

Just like grounding connects you to the Earth, mastering your breath connects you to your inner self, offering a range of health benefits that are both immediate and long-lasting. So, let's take a deeper dive into how mastering the art of breathing can help you attain a state of well-being that complements the benefits you gain from grounding.

Stay tuned, as this chapter lays the groundwork for combining the powers of grounding, early morning sunshine, and deep breathing into an integrated approach to holistic health.

Oxygen and Your Body

Oxygen: The Invisible Catalyst of Life and Well-Being

Oxygen as Cellular Fuel

Often reduced to the simple act of breathing, the role of oxygen in our bodies is far more intricate and indispensable. It acts as a key player in cellular respiration—a biochemical process that allows our cells to convert nutrients into adenosine triphosphate (ATP), the molecular currency of energy in biological systems. In other words, oxygen is to our cells what gasoline is to a car: an essential fuel that powers all functions.

Beyond Breath: The Multi-System Impact of Oxygen

The act of breathing does more than merely fill our lungs; it essentially 'charges' our bodies for optimal performance. A well-oxygenated body can significantly affect the efficacy of organs and systems, from our cardiac activities to our nervous system. Our thought processes become sharper, muscle contractions more efficient, and metabolic rates optimized. This ensures a smoother physiological workflow, from simpler tasks like digesting food to complex functions like neural communication.

The Dark Side of Inadequate Oxygen Levels

The effects of insufficient oxygen levels can be immediate and deleterious. Reduced oxygen intake can lead to sluggishness, both in thought and action. Cognitive capabilities, such as attention, memory, and problem-solving skills, can decline, affecting overall mental performance. In extreme cases, chronic hypoxia—or prolonged lack of sufficient oxygen—can even impair critical bodily functions like cardiac performance and cerebral activities.

THE NEED FOR OXYGEN OPTIMIZATION

Given the overarching role of oxygen in our health, understanding how to maximize oxygen intake becomes a paramount concern for overall well-being. It is not merely a component of respiratory health but a pillar that supports the integrity of multiple bodily systems. Effective oxygenation strategies, therefore, offer a powerful tool for enhancing not only our physical health but also our mental and emotional states.

CONCLUSION

Oxygen isn't just about breathing; it's about living optimally. From the cells to the organ systems, from cognitive functioning to metabolic rates, oxygen serves as an integral component for a wide range of physiological processes. Therefore, proper oxygenation isn't an optional aspect of health; it's a necessity. Learning how to maximize oxygen intake is an invaluable life skill, serving as a cornerstone for comprehensive health and well-being.

THE UNDERESTIMATED POWERHOUSE: UNDERSTANDING AND OPTIMIZING OXYGEN SATURATION

WHAT IS OXYGEN SATURATION?

Oxygen saturation is a medical metric that gauges how effectively your body's red blood cells are loaded with oxygen. Specifically, it measures the percentage of hemoglobin—the oxygen-transporting protein in red blood cells—that is fully occupied with oxygen molecules. The importance of this metric becomes apparent when we consider that oxygen-rich hemoglobin is what enables our cells to perform crucial biological functions, from powering our muscles to enabling cognitive processes.

THE SENTINEL ORGANS: HEART AND BRAIN

When it comes to oxygen, our heart and brain serve as especially sensitive sentinels, requiring consistent and high levels of oxygen saturation for optimum functioning. Fluctuations or decreases in oxygen levels can quickly result in cardiac irregularities and cognitive deficits. It is not an exaggeration to say that maintaining a high level of oxygen saturation is key to the proper functioning of these vital organs.

The Role of Deep Breathing

Traditional shallow chest breathing is far from optimal when it comes to promoting oxygen saturation. In contrast, deep breathing techniques, often referred to as diaphragmatic or belly breathing, facilitate a more comprehensive exchange of gases. This means more oxygen is taken into the body and more carbon dioxide is expelled. As a result, deep breathing significantly improves oxygen saturation levels, ensuring a better delivery of oxygen to cells throughout the body.

A System-wide Impact

Enhanced oxygen saturation isn't just beneficial for isolated physiological functions—it is a critical determinant for the functioning of your body as a whole. From the muscular to the nervous system, higher levels of oxygen saturation ensure that each system can operate at its peak. This makes deep breathing not just a respiratory exercise but a full-body health optimization strategy.

Integrating Oxygen Saturation into a Holistic Well-being Plan

By incorporating deep-breathing exercises into your daily routine, you elevate the entire oxygen supply chain in your body, from the lungs to the smallest capillaries. This proactive approach not only improves each individual breath but also amplifies the effectiveness of the entire respiratory system. In the broader context of well-being, optimal oxygen saturation dovetails perfectly with other pillars of health such as grounding and exposure to early morning sunshine, offering a comprehensive strategy for elevating your overall health and vitality.

CONCLUSION

Oxygen saturation is not merely a metric but a critical indicator of your health and well-being. By understanding its importance and taking actionable steps to optimize it, you open the door to a myriad of health benefits, ranging from improved organ function to enhanced cognitive abilities. It is a simple yet profoundly effective way to uplift your overall health status.

STRESS AND BREATH CONTROL

THE MODERN QUANDARY OF THE "FIGHT OR FLIGHT" RESPONSE: HOW AN EVOLUTIONARY SURVIVAL MECHANISM MISFIRES IN TODAY'S WORLD

WHAT HAPPENS DURING THE "FIGHT OR FLIGHT" RESPONSE?

When your body perceives a threat, the "fight or flight" response kicks in almost instantaneously. This rapid mobilization of resources results in a spike in your heart rate, elevated blood pressure, and increased perspiration. These physiological changes are orchestrated by your body's sympathetic nervous system and adrenal glands, releasing stress hormones like adrenaline and cortisol. These hormones prepare your body for immediate action—either to confront the threat ('fight') or to run away from it ('flight').

THE PHYSIOLOGICAL ADVANTAGE IN A TRUE CRISIS

In the context of genuine life-threatening situations, these physical reactions serve a crucial function. The elevated heart rate and blood pressure ensure that your muscles and vital organs get the increased flow of oxygenated blood they need for peak performance. Essentially, your body is fine-tuned in these moments to help you survive, optimizing your chances of either successfully confronting the threat or fleeing from it.

Misfires in Modern-Day Scenarios

However, the "fight or flight" mechanism isn't well-suited to dealing with the kinds of stress most people encounter today. Whether it's an impending deadline at work, a traffic jam, or a heated disagreement with someone, these are situations where fighting or fleeing are generally not appropriate or effective responses. Unfortunately, your body doesn't differentiate well between these types of stressors and life-threatening ones, often triggering the same full-blown stress response.

The Vicious Cycle of Shallow Breathing

Compounding the issue is the fact that this stress response often comes with shallow, rapid breathing—a pattern that diminishes the efficient exchange of oxygen and carbon dioxide. This inadequate oxygenation can make you feel even more anxious, creating a vicious cycle of tension and stress. Essentially, the very mechanism that's supposed to prepare you for rapid action can end up doing the opposite: it can cloud your thinking, make you more reactive, and drain your emotional resources, rendering you less capable of handling stress effectively.

A Counterproductive Pattern in Modern Stress Management

What we're seeing, then, is an evolutionary survival tactic frequently turned into a counterproductive strategy for managing the more nuanced complexities of modern life. The heightened physiological state, paired with the shallow breathing, often serves to exacerbate our emotional responses to stress, rather than helping us resolve them. This underscores the importance of finding more adaptive ways to cope with the stresses that are an inevitable part of our daily lives.

The Art and Science of Breath Control for Stress Management: Harnessing Your Breath to Counteract the Stress Response

A Toolkit for Breaking the Stress Cycle

The encouraging news is that you don't have to be a passive victim of the stress cycle; you can actively intervene using breath control techniques. These methods serve as practical tools to reverse the physiological and psychological effects of stress, creating a state of balance and calm in the body and mind.

The Mechanics of Diaphragmatic Breathing

One of the fundamental techniques is diaphragmatic breathing, which encourages deeper, slower breaths by engaging the diaphragm, a dome-shaped muscle at the base of your lungs. Instead of shallow chest breathing, diaphragmatic breathing involves expanding the abdomen during inhalation, allowing your lungs to fill more completely with air. This fuller oxygen exchange has a calming effect on the nervous system and can help lower elevated heart rates and blood pressure, effectively reversing many of the negative impacts of the stress response.

The 4-7-8 Technique: A Timed Approach

The 4-7-8 breathing technique offers another potent way to manage stress. The method is simple but highly effective: you inhale through the nose for 4 seconds, hold the breath for 7 seconds, and then exhale fully through the mouth for 8 seconds. The timing is essential, as it helps you focus your mind and provides a structured way to slow down your breathing rate. Scientific research supports the efficacy of this method in significantly reducing stress levels by promoting relaxation and lowering the concentration of stress hormones like cortisol in the blood.

Box Breathing: Symmetry and Balance

Another effective technique is box breathing, so named because it involves four equal parts—inhaling, holding, exhaling, and then holding again, each for the same amount of time. This symmetrical pattern not only slows down the breathing rate but also promotes mental clarity by forcing you to focus on your breath, effectively shutting out distractions and stressors.

Empirical Validation of Controlled Breathing

It's not just anecdotal evidence that supports the effectiveness of these techniques. Multiple scientific studies have shown that controlled breathing can actively lower cortisol levels, induce a state of calm, and significantly improve overall emotional well-being. These methods provide a practical, accessible way to transition from a state of stress to one of relaxation, making them valuable skills in your stress management toolkit.

Conclusion

By mastering the art of breath control, you equip yourself with an immediate, accessible tool to counteract the often maladaptive stress responses triggered by modern life. These techniques not only offer a physiological reset but also pave the way for greater emotional resilience.

The Synergy of Breath and Mindfulness: How Controlled Breathing Enhances Mindful Living

The Breath as a Gateway to Mindfulness

While controlled breathing techniques offer immediate relief from stress, they also serve as a foundational entry point into the broader practice of mindfulness. Focusing intently on each inhalation and exhalation narrows your attention to the present moment, providing a framework for deeper self-awareness. This shift from automatic, shallow breathing to a focused, deliberate breath serves as a gentle introduction to mindfulness, a practice centered on awareness of the present moment without judgment.

The Interplay of Emotional Regulation and Awareness

A cornerstone of mindfulness is emotional regulation—being attuned to your emotions, allowing them to exist without judgment, and not letting them control your actions or thoughts. By focusing your attention on the breath, you cultivate a heightened awareness of your thoughts and feelings, as well as physical sensations, allowing you a more nuanced understanding of your emotional landscape. This increased awareness is integral for emotional regulation and long-term well-being.

Pranayama and Other Breathing Practices: A Rich Tapestry of Techniques

Breathing practices are a staple in various forms of meditation and spiritual exercises. Pranayama, an ancient yogic technique, offers a range of breathing methods designed to control the flow of 'prana' or life force. Each technique serves specific purposes, such as calming the mind, improving focus, or increasing energy. Integrating these advanced breathing exercises can add another layer of richness to your mindfulness practice.

Universal Accessibility: A Tool for All Levels of Practice

One of the most compelling aspects of using breath as a mindfulness tool is its universal applicability. Regardless of your familiarity with mindfulness—whether you're a complete beginner or a seasoned practitioner—controlled breathing serves as a simple yet profoundly effective tool. By just dedicating a few minutes each day to focus on your breath, you can significantly enhance your ability to be fully present, mitigate stress, and gain mental clarity.

A Comprehensive Approach to Well-Being

Mastering the art of controlled breathing not only equips you with a powerful mechanism for stress reduction but also complements other aspects of holistic well-being, such as grounding and absorbing the early morning sunshine, as discussed in previous chapters. These practices, when performed in synergy, contribute to a comprehensive approach to physical and mental health.

In summary, integrating controlled breathing into your mindfulness practice amplifies the benefits of both. This seamless fusion enhances your capacity for present-moment awareness and emotional self-regulation, rounding out a holistic approach to well-being.

CONCLUSION

In this chapter, we've explored the multifaceted benefits of deep breathing, extending beyond mere relaxation to influence vital processes in your body. On one hand, deep breathing enhances the intake of oxygen, a critical element for cellular respiration and energy production. An improved oxygen intake leads to better organ function and contributes to overall health. On the other hand, we delved into the role that controlled breathing plays in mitigating the stress response. By utilizing specific techniques, you can not only reduce stress but also pave the way for mindfulness and emotional regulation.

As you've learned, deep breathing is not an isolated practice but part of a more comprehensive approach to wellness. This sets the stage for the upcoming chapters, where we will guide you through a holistic routine that incorporates all three pillars: grounding, early morning sunshine, and deep breathing. Together, these practices form a synergistic triad that can significantly enhance your health, mood, and well-being.

So, as you turn the page, prepare to learn practical steps to integrate these foundational elements into a transformative daily routine that is both achievable and profoundly impactful.

Chapter 4: Grounding and Your Health

Unlocking the Secrets to Better Sleep and Chronic Pain Relief

As we journey deeper into the transformative practices that contribute to overall health and well-being, it's time to revisit a concept first introduced in Chapter 1: grounding. You'll recall that grounding, or earthing, involves connecting with the Earth's natural electrical energies. It's a practice as ancient as time but backed by modern scientific research.

While the previous chapter gave you a foundational understanding of what grounding is and why it has garnered attention in both traditional practices and scientific communities, this chapter will zoom in on its direct health benefits. More specifically, we will delve into how grounding can improve the quality of your sleep and serve as an effective strategy for chronic pain management.

Prepare to be intrigued and, quite possibly, convinced. The upcoming sections offer a deep dive into the science, testimonials, and case studies that make a compelling case for grounding as not just a wellness trend but as a life-changing practice.

Sleep Quality

The Science of Sleep: Unveiling the Intricate Symphony of Physiological Processes that Shape Your Health

Sleep, often misconceived as a passive state of rest, is actually an active and highly orchestrated physiological event with far-reaching consequences for your health. Contrary to the popular belief that the body and mind "shut down" during sleep, they are, in fact, engaged in a range of complex activities essential for your well-being.

Diving Deeper into the Sleep Cycle

The sleep cycle is a recurring pattern comprising multiple stages, each serving unique roles. Broadly, these are classified into REM (Rapid Eye Movement) sleep and non-REM sleep. REM sleep is particularly intriguing because it is the phase where most dreams occur and is crucial for cognitive functions such as memory consolidation and learning. Non-REM sleep, on the other hand, consists of three stages ranging from light sleep to deep sleep, each facilitating vital restorative processes.

1. **Cellular Repair**: During non-REM deep sleep, your body kicks into high gear to repair and regenerate cells. It's the time when proteins are synthesized, assisting in cellular repair, which is especially important for the immune system, muscles, and various other tissues.

2. **Memory Consolidation**: Throughout the REM phase, your brain sifts through the information acquired during waking hours, storing essential memories and discarding extraneous data. This is key to both academic learning and skill development.

3. **Hormonal Regulation**: Sleep stages also have a significant impact on hormonal balance. For example, growth hormones are primarily released during deep sleep, while cortisol, the stress hormone, tends to decrease during the initial phases of sleep, aiding relaxation and rejuvenation.

The Ripple Effect of Poor Sleep

Insufficient or poor-quality sleep doesn't merely result in fatigue or a bad mood; it can set off a cascade of adverse health effects. A lack of sleep can impair cognitive performance, compromise the immune system, and even disrupt metabolic functions. It can influence your emotional well-being, making you more susceptible to stress, anxiety, and depression.

In essence, sleep is not a monolithic block of time where the body and mind temporarily disengage from the world; it is a dynamic state where critical physiological processes occur in a meticulously coordinated sequence. Understanding this complexity underscores the importance of prioritizing sleep and provides a gateway to appreciate how intricacies like REM and non-REM stages are not just technical jargon but crucial elements that influence your overall health.

Grounding for Better Sleep: How Earth's Natural Rhythms Can Enhance Your Restorative Slumber

The concept of "grounding," or connecting physically with the Earth's surface, has been a subject of increasing interest in the realm of sleep science. Far from being a mere New Age fad, grounding has been empirically linked to improvements in sleep quality, notably in the REM (Rapid Eye Movement) cycle. This aspect of sleep is critical for cognitive functions like memory and learning. What makes grounding so intriguing is its multifaceted approach to enhancing sleep, which incorporates biochemical, physiological, and psychological elements.

The Cortisol Connection

One of the most intriguing findings in grounding research is its impact on cortisol, the body's primary stress hormone. Elevated cortisol levels can severely disrupt sleep architecture, hindering the body's transition into the deep, restorative phases of the sleep cycle. Grounding seems to synchronize cortisol secretion with the natural diurnal rhythms of the Earth, thereby promoting relaxation and facilitating better sleep.

REM Cycle Rejuvenation

Enhanced REM sleep is particularly noteworthy because it's a stage closely associated with mental restoration. Better REM sleep implies improved memory consolidation and enhanced learning capabilities, which can have positive repercussions on daily cognitive functions. Grounding doesn't just aid in falling asleep; it also contributes to the quality of sleep, specifically enriching the REM phase.

Real-world Confirmations: Testimonials and Case Studies

Beyond clinical studies and laboratory data, there's a wealth of anecdotal evidence that underscores the effectiveness of grounding. Testimonials from individuals who have incorporated grounding into their nightly routines frequently mention not just quicker sleep onset but also deeper, more fulfilling sleep. These firsthand accounts serve to validate scientific hypotheses, making the case for grounding even more compelling.

Far-reaching Implications for Health and Well-being

The improvement in sleep quality through grounding is not just a standalone benefit; it has ripple effects that influence your overall health. Better sleep, enriched by grounding practices, contributes to more balanced hormonal levels, improved cognitive function, and a more robust immune system, among other health benefits.

In summary, grounding offers a unique and scientifically substantiated method to not only help you fall asleep but also to enrich the quality of your sleep. Its multi-level impact—from hormonal regulation to cognitive improvement—provides yet another compelling reason to integrate this practice into your daily life.

Chronic Pain Reduction

The Multifaceted Reality of Chronic Pain: A Deeper Dive into Its Complexity and Psychological Impact

The phenomenon of pain is not monolithic; it presents itself in a variety of forms and intensities, each with its unique set of implications. While acute pain is more straightforward, often serving as a body's natural alert system to injury or illness, chronic pain is far more insidious and complicated. Unlike acute pain, which usually fades as the body heals, chronic pain can extend for prolonged periods—lasting weeks, months, or even years.

Not Just Physical Suffering

The traditional understanding of pain as merely a physical sensation does not apply to chronic pain, which transcends this dimension to become a comprehensive, often debilitating, experience. The longevity of chronic pain does not just result in physical discomfort; it exacts a toll on a person's psychological well-being as well.

The Mental Health Cascade

One of the most underemphasized aspects of chronic pain is its capacity to significantly diminish mental health. Persistent pain often serves as a catalyst for conditions such as depression and anxiety, as the relentless discomfort makes normal life increasingly challenging. The pain, in essence, becomes both a physical and emotional burden that clouds every aspect of daily living.

The Quality of Life Quagmire

Perhaps one of the most devastating impacts of chronic pain is its effect on one's quality of life. Routine activities that were once taken for granted may become Herculean tasks. Social interactions can decline as the sufferer withdraws, partly because of the physical pain and partly due to the accompanying psychological stressors.

A Cycle of Suffering

The intertwining of physical and psychological suffering in chronic pain creates a vicious cycle. The physical pain exacerbates mental health issues, which in turn can intensify the perception of pain. This cyclical nature makes treating chronic pain especially complex because healthcare providers must address not just the physiological aspects but also the accompanying emotional and psychological facets.

In summary, chronic pain is not a stand-alone symptom but rather a multifaceted condition that wreaks havoc on both physical and mental health. Its long-lasting nature and the complex interplay between the physical and psychological aspects make it one of the most challenging medical conditions to manage effectively.

Grounding as a Frontier in Chronic Pain Management: Unveiling the Science and Real-world Outcomes

The concept of grounding, sometimes referred to as "Earthing," is emerging as an intriguing and scientifically backed approach in the realm of chronic pain management. While traditional medical interventions often focus on pharmaceuticals and surgical procedures, grounding offers a more natural, holistic method that has shown promise in both scientific studies and real-world applications.

Anti-Inflammatory Mechanism: The Biological Rationale

One of the central scientific theories supporting grounding's effectiveness in pain management is its ability to modulate inflammation. Chronic inflammation is frequently implicated in persistent pain conditions, be it arthritis, fibromyalgia, or neuropathic pain. Grounding appears to act as a normalizing force for certain inflammatory markers within the body. Through complex biochemical processes, grounding may help to neutralize free radicals and reduce oxidative stress, factors often associated with inflammation. This cascade of biochemical events has the potential to mitigate the symptoms and intensity of chronic pain, offering sufferers a tangible relief mechanism.

Real-world Evidence: Case Studies and Testimonials

The scientific underpinnings of grounding are further bolstered by anecdotal evidence and case studies. Individuals incorporating grounding techniques into their wellness routines have reported tangible reductions in chronic pain levels across a spectrum of conditions—from lower back pain to migraines. This lived experience resonates strongly, particularly for those who have found little relief from conventional treatments.

A Comprehensive Approach: Beyond Just Pain

Another noteworthy aspect is grounding's ability to improve the overall quality of life. By mitigating chronic pain, grounding doesn't merely alleviate physical suffering; it often paves the way for greater mobility, improved sleep, and enhanced mental well-being. As a result, those who adopt grounding techniques not only experience pain reduction but also enjoy a more holistic improvement in their health and lifestyle.

Filling in the Gaps of Traditional Treatment

Grounding's unique advantages become particularly relevant when conventional treatments fall short or produce undesirable side effects. For those seeking alternatives or supplementary approaches, grounding serves as an appealing, non-invasive option that can be easily incorporated into daily routines.

In conclusion, grounding is emerging as a potent tool in the chronic pain management toolkit. Its potential benefits are grounded (pun intended) in both science and real-world outcomes, making it a compelling alternative or addition to traditional methods of pain management.

Conclusion

Grounding, as we've explored, is not just a new-age concept but a scientifically supported practice with tangible health benefits. Particularly, it can be a game-changer in two critical areas of wellness: improving sleep quality and reducing chronic pain. Studies have indicated that grounding can lead to better REM cycles, contributing to more restorative sleep. Likewise, its anti-inflammatory effects can be a boon for chronic pain sufferers, offering a natural and effective pathway to pain relief.

As you turn the page, we'll bask in the light of our next significant topic—early morning sunshine. Just like grounding, the first rays of the day have their unique set of health benefits that could make a difference in your life. So, let's journey from the ground to the sky to continue our exploration into holistic health.

CHAPTER 5: EARLY MORNING SUNSHINE FOR WELLBEING

Illuminating Wellness: How Morning Sunshine Elevates Mood and Revitalizes Skin

In the previous chapter, we delved into the scientific underpinnings of early morning sunshine, unraveling its myriad benefits. We learned how the first rays of the day can do more than just light up the sky; they can light up our lives in unexpected ways. But we've only scratched the surface. In this chapter, we will zero in on two particular aspects that could profoundly change your well-being: mood enhancement and skin health.

We'll explore how early morning sunlight can positively interact with neurotransmitters in the brain to uplift your mood. We'll also dive into the growing body of evidence that suggests that morning sun exposure can be beneficial for various skin conditions. So let's delve deeper into how this natural gift of morning sunshine can contribute to a happier, healthier you.

Mood Enhancement

The Sun as Nature's Antidepressant: Understanding the Biochemistry of Mood Enhancement and Seasonal Affective Disorder

It's often said that sunshine can bring a smile to your face, but the effects of sun exposure on mood are not merely poetic or anecdotal—they're scientific facts. The sun, particularly its morning rays, serves as a natural mood booster, impacting the neurochemical landscape of our brains in significant ways.

Serotonin: The "Feel-Good" Neurotransmitter

One of the key players in this biochemical interaction is serotonin, often dubbed the "feel-good hormone" or "happy chemical." This neurotransmitter is crucial for mood regulation, and its levels in the brain can be directly influenced by sunlight exposure. When the sun's rays hit the skin, a sequence of biochemical reactions leads to the conversion of tryptophan to serotonin. Elevated levels of serotonin are associated with feelings of well-being, relaxation, and focus. The process isn't merely anecdotal or folklore; it's supported by a wealth of scientific studies.

Seasonal Affective Disorder (SAD): A Case Study for Sunlight's Effectiveness

The role of morning sunlight becomes even more pivotal when we consider Seasonal Affective Disorder (SAD), a form of depression characterized by mood changes that align with seasonal variations. During the winter months, when daylight is scarce, individuals suffering from SAD often experience exacerbations in depressive symptoms. Conversely, these symptoms often alleviate with increased exposure to sunlight. The science suggests that morning sunlight can reset the circadian rhythm, a natural internal process that regulates the sleep-wake cycle, and helps to release mood-enhancing neurotransmitters like serotonin. Essentially, the sun acts as a natural antidote to the seasonal blues.

A Role in Circadian Rhythm

The circadian rhythm, our internal biological clock, is highly sensitive to light and dark. Morning sunlight can act as a "reset" button for our circadian rhythms, thus affecting not just our mood but also other physiological processes like sleep quality and metabolic rate. By helping to recalibrate this biological clock, morning sunlight aids in more than just mood enhancement; it contributes to a general sense of well-being and vitality.

In conclusion, the relationship between sunlight and mood is far more than a cultural or poetic metaphor. It is a scientifically backed interaction that has profound implications for mental health, from boosting levels of serotonin to acting as a natural remedy against

Seasonal Affective Disorder. Morning sunlight, it seems, is a natural prescription for a brighter outlook on life.

Illuminating the Science: A Closer Look at Studies and Evidence on Morning Sunlight and Mood Enhancement

Academic Research: Peer-Reviewed Studies

One of the most compelling pieces of evidence comes from academic research. For example, a noteworthy study published in the journal "Environmental Health Perspectives" specifically explored the relationship between morning sunlight exposure and depression. The researchers found a significant correlation: individuals who were exposed to larger amounts of morning sunlight exhibited lower levels of depression compared to those who had little to no exposure. This wasn't an isolated study; several other research papers have corroborated these findings, emphasizing the scientific consensus on sunlight's mood-boosting properties.

Real-Life Testimonials: The Human Element

Beyond the world of academic journals, real-world testimonials and case studies offer valuable qualitative insights into the mood-enhancing effects of morning sunlight. Numerous individuals have reported marked improvements in their mental well-being after incorporating simple sun-centric practices into their daily routines. A prime example is the transformative power of a 20-minute morning walk. People who adopted this straightforward habit noted feeling not just happier but also more focused and less anxious. These first-hand accounts serve as compelling, personalized evidence that complements the more quantitative data from scientific studies.

Mobile Apps and Tracking Tools: Quantifying Mood Improvements

In the era of digital health, mobile apps designed to track mood and mental well-being are providing additional data points that back the science of sun-induced mood enhancement. Users who log their mood scores before and after adopting a routine of morning sunlight exposure often see a quantifiable increase in positive mood metrics. These digital tools add another layer of credibility to the existing body of evidence, allowing for a more nuanced understanding of how sunlight affects mood at an individual level.

INTERDISCIPLINARY APPROACHES: NEUROSCIENCE AND PSYCHOLOGY

The mood-boosting effects of sunlight are not only recognized in the fields of environmental health or epidemiology but also garner attention in neuroscience and psychology. These disciplines explore the neurochemical changes induced by sunlight, further affirming the biochemical relationship between sun exposure and serotonin levels, among other neurotransmitters.

In summary, the weight of the evidence—be it from peer-reviewed studies, real-life testimonials, or interdisciplinary research—strongly confirms the positive impact of morning sunlight on mood. It serves as a natural, yet powerful, remedy for mood enhancement, and its benefits are supported both anecdotally and scientifically.

SKIN HEALTH

SUNSHINE AND SKIN

Sunlight doesn't just lift your spirits; it can also do wonders for your skin when approached mindfully. Moderate exposure to early morning sunlight has been shown to have therapeutic effects on various skin conditions, including acne and psoriasis. The UV rays in the morning are less intense compared to the harsh midday sun, making it a safer time for sun exposure with minimal risk of skin damage.

Research suggests that UVB rays from the sun can actually help alleviate symptoms of psoriasis by slowing down the rapid growth of skin cells. Additionally, morning sunlight can stimulate the production of Vitamin D, which plays a role in skin health and can aid in the management of acne through its anti-inflammatory properties.

Striking the Perfect Balance: Navigating Vitamin D Synthesis and Skin Protection in Sunlight Exposure

Time Management: Your First Line of Defense

The adage "timing is everything" couldn't be more accurate when it comes to sun exposure. Experts generally recommend limiting your sun time to 10-30 minutes in the early morning when the sun's rays are less harsh. This window allows you to absorb necessary UVB rays for Vitamin D production without overexposing your skin to potential harm. However, this time frame can fluctuate based on your skin type and geographical location. For example, those living closer to the equator may need to reduce their sun exposure time due to the sun's increased intensity.

Sunscreen: A Double-Edged Sword

Sunscreen is indispensable for preventing skin damage during extended periods of sun exposure. Using a broad-spectrum sunscreen with at least SPF 30 is the go-to advice. However, it's important to recognize that sunscreen can also inhibit Vitamin D synthesis. The conundrum, then, is how to protect your skin while still benefiting from the sun's rays. The solution? Go sunscreen-free for short durations, specifically in the early morning. This allows for Vitamin D synthesis without significantly increasing the risk of skin damage.

Skin Type Specifics: Tailoring Your Sun Strategy

Your skin type is another critical factor in this balancing act. Lighter skin types synthesize Vitamin D more quickly but are also more susceptible to skin damage. These individuals might aim for the lower end of the 10-30 minute recommendation for sun exposure. In contrast, those with darker skin types are more resilient to UV rays but may require a longer exposure time to produce adequate levels of Vitamin

D. Customizing your sun exposure strategy based on your skin type can maximize benefits while minimizing risks.

SMART TOOLS AND WEARABLES: TECH TO THE RESCUE

Today's smart wearables and skin-monitoring apps offer an additional layer of guidance. These tools can provide real-time data about UV intensity and alert you when it's time to head for shade or apply sunscreen, helping you navigate the fine line between adequate Vitamin D synthesis and skin protection effectively.

INTEGRATING WITH SKINCARE REGIMENS

Incorporating this balanced approach to sun exposure can seamlessly fit into broader skincare routines. For instance, applying a vitamin C serum before your limited sun exposure can offer some photoprotection, while a good after-sun lotion can help repair any potential UV damage.

In summary, achieving better skin health through sun exposure is not a matter of all-or-nothing. It's about understanding the nuances and striking a balance. With smart time management, judicious use of sunscreen, and a tailored approach based on skin type, you can enjoy the spectrum of sun-derived benefits without compromising skin health.

CONCLUSION

In this chapter, we've illuminated the multi-faceted benefits of early morning sunshine. From enhancing neurotransmitters like serotonin that play a crucial role in mood regulation to its therapeutic effects on skin conditions such as acne and psoriasis, the morning sun offers more than just a beautiful start to the day. It serves as a natural remedy for elevating mental well-being and improving skin health.

As we wrap up this enlightening journey into the power of the morning sun, let's prepare to shift our focus from external rays to the inner rhythm of our breath. The next chapter will dive deep into the transformative art of deep breathing, exploring how mastering this simple yet profound act can bring mental clarity and serve as a potent tool for stress reduction.

By marrying the external benefits of morning sunshine with the internal control of breath, you'll be well-equipped to face each day with a harmonious blend of mental clarity and emotional balance. Stay tuned.

Chapter 6: Deep Breathing and Mindfulness

Breathing with Intent: Unpacking the Cognitive and Mindfulness Benefits of Deep Breathing

In Chapter 3, we delved into the science of deep breathing, examining how this simple yet powerful act affects oxygen intake and stress regulation. We explored the physiological changes brought about by deep breathing and discussed its immediate health benefits. As we move forward, this chapter aims to deepen your understanding of deep breathing by shining a light on its cognitive and mindfulness aspects.

This isn't just about inhaling and exhaling; it's about weaving the practice into the fabric of your daily life to not only manage stress but also to elevate your mental faculties. We will look at how specific breathing techniques can help to calm the nervous system and delve into the science that confirms why these practices are effective for reducing anxiety. Additionally, we'll explore how mindfulness coupled with deep breathing can lead to significant improvements in cognitive functions like focus, memory, and decision-making.

In essence, this chapter serves as your guide to comprehending the mental and cognitive dimensions of deep breathing, rounding out your understanding and equipping you with the tools to lead a more balanced and mindful life.

ANXIETY AND STRESS REDUCTION

BREATHING TECHNIQUES FOR CALMNESS

In our daily lives, stress and anxiety often seem like unavoidable companions. However, the key to reclaiming your peace could be as simple as taking a deep breath—literally. In this section, we'll delve into specific breathing techniques known to induce calmness and alleviate stress.

UNPACKING DIAPHRAGMATIC BREATHING: A DEEP DIVE INTO THE PHYSIOLOGY AND BENEFITS OF A SIMPLE STRESS-RELIEF TECHNIQUE

ANATOMY OF A BREATH: DIAPHRAGM VS. CHEST BREATHING

Breathing is such an automatic activity that most of us rarely give it much thought. However, not all breathing is created equal. In chest breathing, we engage the muscles in our chest and shoulders, taking shallow breaths that don't fully utilize our lung capacity. In contrast, diaphragmatic breathing focuses on the diaphragm, a dome-shaped muscle located just below the lungs. By consciously engaging the diaphragm, we can take deeper, fuller breaths, which result in a more effective exchange of oxygen and carbon dioxide.

THE PHYSIOLOGY OF CALM: OXYGEN EXCHANGE AND ITS IMPACT

The quality of our breathing has a direct effect on our physiology. A deep, diaphragmatic breath encourages full oxygen exchange—an essential process that improves the oxygenation of our blood. This in turn can slow down your heartbeat and stabilize blood pressure, which sends cues to the brain to activate the parasympathetic nervous system, often referred to as the "rest and digest" system. The resulting shift in your nervous system promotes a calming effect, decreasing feelings of stress and anxiety.

Triggering the Relaxation Response: How It Works

When you practice diaphragmatic breathing, you engage the vagus nerve, a crucial nerve that originates in the brain and plays a major role in regulating various body functions including mood. The activation of the vagus nerve prompts the release of neurotransmitters like acetylcholine, which helps dampen the stress response. This aids in reducing the levels of cortisol, the stress hormone, contributing to a more relaxed state of being.

Measurable Health Benefits: What the Data Says

While anecdotal evidence of the calming effect of diaphragmatic breathing abounds, scientific studies also corroborate its effectiveness. Research has shown that individuals who practice diaphragmatic breathing experience lower levels of stress hormones, improved mood, and even better cognitive performance. For instance, a study published in the "Journal of Clinical Psychology" noted significant reductions in symptoms of stress and anxiety among participants who engaged in deep-breathing exercises, such as diaphragmatic breathing.

Practical Application: Making Diaphragmatic Breathing a Habit

Implementing diaphragmatic breathing into your daily routine is surprisingly straightforward. Here are some steps to get you started:

1. **Find a Quiet Space:** Choose a quiet, comfortable place where you won't be disturbed.

2. **Positioning:** Sit or lie down, placing one hand on your chest and the other on your abdomen.

3. **Inhale:** Breathe in deeply through the nose, focusing on expanding your diaphragm rather than lifting your chest.

4. **Exhale:** Release the breath slowly through the mouth or nose, noting the descent of the diaphragm.

5. **Repetition:** Aim for at least 5-10 deep breaths, working your way up as you become more comfortable with the technique.

Mastering diaphragmatic breathing doesn't just offer immediate relief; it provides a long-term strategy for managing stress and enhancing your emotional well-being. It's a simple yet profoundly effective tool that you can deploy at any time, wherever you are.

The 4-7-8 Breathing Method: Unlocking the Secrets of a Time-Bound Technique for Instant Calm

The Rhythm of Breathing: A Structured Approach

4-7-8 breathing is a structured breathing technique that offers a straightforward yet powerful way to combat stress and anxiety. Unlike more freestyle methods, this technique relies on a specific rhythm: inhale for 4 seconds, hold the breath for 7 seconds, and exhale for 8 seconds. This regimen sets it apart and is the key to its effectiveness.

Prolonged Breath-Holding: The Key to Relaxation

The unique aspect of the 4-7-8 method is the prolonged breath-holding phase, which lasts for 7 seconds. During this period, your body has more time to take in oxygen, and the longer exhalation helps to remove more carbon dioxide. This pause or holding of the breath acts as a "reset button" for the nervous system, helping to trigger the relaxation response. The result is an effective calming of the nervous system, reducing stress hormones and promoting a sense of well-being.

Neurological Mechanisms: The Science Behind the Calm

When you engage in 4-7-8 breathing, the extended breath-holding and exhalation phases activate the parasympathetic nervous system, commonly known as the "rest and digest" system. This shift in the nervous system landscape results in a decrease in heart rate and blood pressure, creating an immediate sense of calm. Scientifically, this form of breathing stimulates the vagus nerve, facilitating a decrease in the release of stress hormones like cortisol.

How it Stands Up to Research

While the technique may seem simplistic, its impact is backed by science. Numerous studies have demonstrated that controlled breathing techniques, including the 4-7-8 method, effectively reduce stress and anxiety. For example, a study published in the Journal of Clinical Psychology showed that participants practicing breath control techniques experienced measurable reductions in stress indicators.

Practical Tips for Implementing 4-7-8 Breathing

1. **Find a Quiet Space:** Choose an environment where you can focus without distraction.

2. **Get Comfortable:** Whether seated or lying down, make sure you're in a comfortable position.

3. **Follow the Pattern:** Inhale through the nose for 4 seconds, hold the breath for 7 seconds, and exhale through the mouth for 8 seconds.

4. **Repeat:** Try to complete at least four cycles initially, and gradually increase as you get more accustomed to the practice.

In summary, the 4-7-8 breathing technique is not just an age-old adage but a scientifically supported method for immediate stress relief. Its rigid structure and extended breath-holding phase make it a quick and effective tool for calming the nervous system and improving your emotional well-being.

The Art of Box Breathing: Creating a Symphony of Calm in Four Equal Parts

A Square Solution for Stress: The 'Box' Concept

Box breathing is aptly named for its structured approach to stress management, mimicking the symmetry of a square or a box. This involves four equal phases: inhaling, holding the breath, exhaling, and holding the breath again, each typically lasting for four seconds. This sequence forms a 'box,' providing a highly organized structure that serves as a reliable framework for bringing the mind and body back to equilibrium.

Resetting the Nervous System: A Balanced Approach

One of the most remarkable aspects of box breathing is its ability to "reset" the nervous system. Each of the four phases serves a specific physiological purpose. The inhalation fills the lungs with oxygen, which is critical for every cell in the body. The first hold allows this oxygen to spread throughout the bloodstream. Exhalation serves to remove carbon dioxide, a waste product. The final hold serves to stabilize the respiratory system before the next inhalation. This orchestrated set of actions engages the parasympathetic nervous system, also known as the "rest and digest" system, counterbalancing the sympathetic "fight or flight" system activated by stress.

Neurobiological Underpinnings: It's More Than Just Air

Scientifically, box breathing seems to have a profound impact on the nervous system by stimulating the vagus nerve. This important nerve plays a crucial role in regulating stress response, heart rate, and digestion among other functions. When activated through slow, conscious breathing, the vagus nerve sends signals to the brain to turn down the stress response, leading to a decrease in heart rate and a feeling of calm.

Tried and Tested: Why it Works

This technique has found its advocates among high-stress professions, including Navy SEALs, first responders, and medical professionals. Moreover, its effectiveness is backed by various studies that have highlighted the impact of paced breathing techniques, like box breathing, in reducing stress and anxiety symptoms. For instance, a study in the "Journal of Clinical Psychology" indicated that breathing exercises could be a potent non-pharmacological intervention for reducing stress and anxiety.

Tips for Mastering Box Breathing

1. **Find Your Space:** Choose a quiet, comfortable location where you can focus entirely on your breath.

2. **Position Yourself:** Whether sitting or lying down, ensure you are relaxed and your posture is neutral.

3. **Follow the Square:** Inhale, hold, exhale, hold—each for a count of four. Visualizing a square as you do this can help keep you focused.

4. **Be Consistent:** For maximum benefit, make it a regular practice, aiming for at least a few minutes per session to start.

In conclusion, box breathing is not just a mental exercise but a holistic approach to resetting your nervous system. Its four equally important phases work in harmony to bring about a state of calm and focus, making it an effective tool for stress relief backed by both practice and science.

Each of these techniques serves to engage the parasympathetic nervous system, often called the "rest and digest" system, making them potent tools for calming your mind and body.

The Science of Calm

You're not just imagining that sigh of relief that comes after a deep breath; it's backed by science. Deep, mindful breathing triggers neurological and hormonal changes that promote a state of calm and relaxation.

The Neurological Symphony of Deep Breathing: Tuning the Vagus Nerve for Calm

The Central Role of the Vagus Nerve

One of the most significant players in the deep breathing process is the vagus nerve, a sprawling neural highway that originates in the brain and extends down to the abdomen, connecting various internal organs along its route. Considered one of the most critical nerves in the body, the vagus nerve acts as the central hub for regulating a wide array of physiological functions, from digestion to heart rate.

Activation Through Deep Breathing

When you engage in deep, mindful breathing, you are essentially flipping the activation switch on your vagus nerve. This nerve is particularly sensitive to changes in breathing patterns. When activated, it serves as a conduit, sending specific 'calm down and relax' signals to different parts of the body.

The Neurochemical Cascade: Acetylcholine and Beyond

Upon activation through deep breathing, the vagus nerve prompts the release of various neurotransmitters, with acetylcholine being among the most notable. Acetylcholine acts like a molecular messenger with a soothing agenda. Its primary role is to slow down the rate of heartbeat and encourage smooth muscle relaxation, essentially guiding the body into a more peaceful, restorative state.

The Calming Effect: More than Just a Feeling

The release of acetylcholine has a potent calming effect on the nervous system. This action is not merely a fleeting moment of relaxation but a physiologically mediated shift that aids in reducing stress, anxiety, and inflammation. Moreover, the stimulation of the vagus nerve has been shown to improve conditions ranging from depression to digestive disorders, further illustrating the multifaceted benefits of this neural pathway.

Scientific Backing: The Research Landscape

The calming effects of vagus nerve activation through deep breathing aren't just theoretical—they're supported by a wealth of scientific evidence. Studies in neurophysiology and psychology have consistently shown that the activation of the vagus nerve can lead to improved mental health outcomes, including reduced levels of stress and anxiety.

In summary, the neurological changes instigated by deep breathing are profound and impactful, serving as a natural and effective method for stress management. Through the activation of the vagus nerve and the subsequent release of calming neurotransmitters like acetylcholine, deep breathing offers a scientifically supported avenue for achieving mental calm and well-being.

The Hormonal Harmony of Deep Breathing: Lowering Cortisol to Cultivate Calm

Cortisol: The Stress Hormone

Cortisol is often dubbed the "stress hormone" due to its crucial role in the body's "fight or flight" response—a physiological reaction to perceived threats. While cortisol is beneficial in short bursts, such as helping you escape danger, chronic elevation of this hormone can lead to negative health effects like increased anxiety, sleep problems, and even chronic diseases like hypertension.

The Deep Breathing Connection

Deep breathing exercises have a direct influence on the hormonal balance in your body. When you engage in practices like diaphragmatic breathing, 4-7-8 breathing, or box breathing, the act itself serves as a biological cue that triggers the endocrine system to lower cortisol levels.

Biochemical Pathways: Cortisol and Deep Breathing

The mechanism behind this involves the hypothalamic pituitary adrenal (HPA) axis, a complex set of direct influences and feedback interactions among the hypothalamus, the pituitary gland, and the adrenal glands. Deep breathing prompts these glands to produce less cortisol, in effect dampening the stress response.

The Result: A State of Calm

As cortisol levels decrease, you are more likely to experience a state of calmness and relaxation. Lower cortisol levels are linked to a range of health benefits including improved mood, better sleep quality, and even a stronger immune system. The lowering of cortisol also works synergistically with the activation of the vagus nerve, amplifying the body's relaxation response.

A Body of Evidence: Scientific Research

The hormonal changes induced by deep breathing aren't merely anecdotal; they are backed by a robust body of scientific literature. Numerous studies have shown that participants practicing regular deep breathing exercises experience a significant reduction in cortisol levels, thereby validating the hormonal pathway through which deep breathing manifests its calming effects.

In summary, the hormonal changes facilitated by deep breathing—particularly the reduction in cortisol levels—constitute a crucial component in its efficacy as a stress-reduction tool. By understanding and leveraging these hormonal shifts, individuals can gain an additional, scientifically grounded technique for achieving emotional equilibrium and better overall health.

Enhanced Cognitive Function

The Brain on Deep Breathing

The benefits of deep breathing aren't confined solely to stress relief; they extend into the realms of cognitive enhancement as well. A well-oxygenated brain is a high-functioning brain. When you engage in deep breathing, more oxygen reaches your brain cells, improving various cognitive faculties.

The Focus Factor: How Deep Breathing Oxygenates Your Brain for Enhanced Concentration

The Biology of Brain Function and Oxygen

The brain is a remarkably energy-demanding organ, consuming about 20% of the body's total oxygen and nutrients. The biochemical process of energy production in the brain is highly dependent on a steady supply of oxygen. In essence, the more oxygen that reaches your brain cells, the more efficiently they can produce the energy needed for various cognitive tasks, including concentration.

Oxygen and Neurotransmitter Activity

Oxygen also plays a pivotal role in the synthesis of neurotransmitters, the chemical messengers that facilitate communication between neurons. A well-oxygenated brain facilitates the optimal function of neurotransmitters like dopamine and norepinephrine, which are essential for focus and attention. Insufficient oxygen, on the other hand, can lead to reduced neurotransmitter activity and subsequently poor concentration.

Deep Breathing: A Simple Solution

Engaging in deep breathing exercises like diaphragmatic breathing or the 4-7-8 technique ensures a more substantial influx of oxygen into your bloodstream, which is then efficiently delivered to the brain. The deeper you breathe, the more oxygen-rich blood reaches the brain, enabling higher energy production and improved neurotransmitter activity.

Immediate and Sustained Effects

The benefits of deep breathing on concentration can be both immediate and long-lasting. Even short bouts of deep breathing exercises can yield noticeable improvements in your ability to focus on tasks at hand. For sustained benefits, making deep breathing a daily practice can lead to lasting improvements in concentration and overall cognitive function.

Real-world Implications

This isn't merely theoretical; the increased capacity for concentration has tangible effects in everyday life. Whether you're a student aiming for higher academic performance, a professional juggling multiple responsibilities, or an athlete striving for peak performance, enhanced focus is a universally beneficial asset. It can mean the difference between achieving your goals and falling short.

In summary, deep breathing serves as a simple yet potent tool for improving concentration. By ensuring your brain is well-oxygenated, you equip yourself with a greater ability to focus, thereby optimizing performance across various domains of life.

The Memory Connection: How Oxygen Levels Influence Neurotransmitter Function for Enhanced Recall

The Physiology of Memory and Oxygen

Memory is a complex cognitive function involving various brain regions and neurotransmitter systems. Neurons—the cells that transmit information in the brain—rely on an adequate supply of oxygen to perform their functions effectively. Neurotransmitters like acetylcholine and glutamate, which play vital roles in memory formation and retrieval, require optimal conditions for synthesis and signaling. One of those conditions is adequate oxygenation.

Oxygen and Memory Mechanisms

Neurotransmitters operate as part of intricate signaling pathways that facilitate the formation of memories in the hippocampus, storage in other brain regions, and retrieval when needed. Oxygen is crucial for enzymatic reactions that synthesize these neurotransmitters, as well as for the mitochondrial processes that provide the energy for neurotransmitter release and signaling. A well-oxygenated environment thus enables the neurotransmitter systems to work at their peak capacity, aiding memory retention and recall.

The Detrimental Effects of Low Oxygen Levels

When the brain receives insufficient oxygen, neurons struggle to perform their duties, leading to inefficient neurotransmitter signaling. This inefficiency impacts the encoding and retrieval of memories, making tasks like recall and recognition significantly more challenging. Low oxygen levels may also lead to cognitive fog, further hampering memory function.

Implementing Deep Breathing for Memory Improvement

Given the relationship between oxygen and memory, it stands to reason that improving oxygen levels through deep breathing exercises can have a beneficial impact on memory functions. Techniques like diaphragmatic breathing, 4-7-8 breathing, or box breathing can help ensure that enough oxygen-rich blood is reaching your brain, thereby creating an optimal environment for neurotransmitter function.

Everyday Implications and Long-term Benefits

The potential benefits are wide-ranging, from recalling names and dates more easily to enhancing academic performance. For older adults, maintaining optimal brain oxygenation could even contribute to delaying cognitive decline, including memory loss.

In summary, by understanding the deep connection between oxygen levels and neurotransmitter function, you can leverage deep breathing exercises as a practical tool for enhancing memory retention and recall. Through conscious control of your breathing, you have the power to optimize your cognitive functions, including the intricate processes involved in memory.

Navigating Choices: How Enhanced Oxygen Levels Optimize Neurotransmitter Activity for Superior Decision-making

The Neural Basis of Decision-making

Decision-making is a multi-faceted cognitive process that involves evaluating options, assessing risks and rewards, and ultimately selecting an action. This complex task requires the orchestrated function of various brain regions, such as the prefrontal cortex, which is responsible for executive functions. Just like any other neural process, the efficacy of decision-making is highly dependent on the optimal functioning of neurotransmitters and brain cells, which in turn, rely on adequate oxygen supply.

Oxygen: The Fuel for Better Decisions

Oxygen serves as a critical fuel for brain cells, enabling them to generate the energy required for neurotransmitter production, release, and reuptake. Improved oxygen levels result in heightened neuronal activity and a more efficient signaling process. This elevated state allows for a quicker and more effective evaluation of situations, enhancing your decision-making abilities. Whether it's choosing between career paths or deciding on a course of action in a high-stakes situation, a well-oxygenated brain is more adept at processing the variables and making a reasoned choice.

The Role of Neurotransmitters

Neurotransmitters like dopamine and serotonin play vital roles in decision-making. Dopamine, for instance, is crucial for weighing the rewards of different choices, while serotonin affects risk assessment. A better-oxygenated brain can synthesize these neurotransmitters more effectively, allowing for a more balanced and nuanced approach to decision-making.

Deep Breathing: The Pathway to Improved Decision-making

Implementing deep breathing techniques into your routine can offer a practical method for boosting your brain's oxygen levels. By taking deep, deliberate breaths, you enhance the oxygenation of your blood, which directly impacts your brain's performance. As a result, you may find that you are better equipped to make sound decisions, whether in the workplace, at school, or in your personal life.

Beyond the Immediate Choice

The benefits of improved decision-making are not just limited to individual situations; they can have a cascading effect on various aspects of your life. Good decisions compound over time, leading to improved outcomes in career advancement, relationship building, and overall well-being.

In summary, sufficient oxygenation of the brain can significantly improve neurotransmitter activity and general neuronal function, providing a natural way to enhance your decision-making skills. By incorporating deep breathing exercises into your daily routine, you are taking proactive steps to optimize your cognitive abilities, including the intricate processes involved in making decisions.

Alongside these cognitive benefits, deep breathing exercises often serve as the foundation for mindfulness practices that further augment cognitive function.

The Empirical Backbone: Unveiling the Robust Evidence Supporting Deep Breathing for Cognitive Enhancement

The Academic Lens: Journal of Cognitive Enhancement

The relationship between deep breathing and cognitive performance isn't merely theoretical; it is well-supported by empirical evidence. One of the notable contributions to this body of research is a study published in the Journal of Cognitive Enhancement. This study lends significant credence to the notion that deep breathing and mindfulness practices can positively impact cognitive functions like working memory and executive function. These are key abilities that influence various aspects of our lives, from problem-solving to planning and multitasking. The study's findings go beyond anecdotal claims, offering scientific validation for the cognitive benefits of deep breathing exercises.

Corporate Adoption: Google and Apple Lead the Way

In the realm of business, where productivity and decision-making are paramount, some of the world's leading corporations have recognized the value of deep breathing and mindfulness. Google and Apple, known for their innovative approaches to employee well-being, have integrated these practices into their corporate wellness programs. Both companies have reported measurable improvements in productivity and decision-making skills among employees who participated in mindfulness and deep breathing sessions. This corporate endorsement serves as a strong indicator of the efficacy of deep breathing techniques for cognitive enhancement, bridging the gap between scientific research and real-world application.

Anecdotal Accounts: Students and Athletes

While scientific studies and corporate practices provide strong evidence, anecdotal experiences add another layer of support. Students who have adopted deep breathing exercises as part of their pre-exam routines have reported marked improvements in academic performance. Similarly, athletes who focus on mindful breathing have noted enhanced concentration during games, which subsequently leads to improved overall performance. These firsthand accounts, although not as rigorously controlled as scientific studies, offer valuable insights into the practical benefits of deep breathing for cognitive function.

THE CONFLUENCE OF EVIDENCE

Taken together, these multiple lines of evidence—academic research, corporate initiatives, and anecdotal experiences—form a compelling case for the cognitive advantages of deep breathing. Whether you are aiming to advance in your professional sphere, excel in academics, or improve your athletic performance, incorporating deep breathing techniques into your daily routine can significantly enhance your cognitive abilities. The scientific and anecdotal evidence suggests that deep breathing is not merely a relaxation tool but a catalyst for unlocking your full cognitive potential.

CONCLUSION

Deep breathing, especially when practiced mindfully, serves as a multifaceted tool for well-being. Not only does it significantly reduce anxiety by calming the nervous system, but it also offers cognitive benefits that can improve your quality of life. From enhanced focus and memory to better decision-making, deep breathing has the power to positively impact mental clarity and function.

This chapter sets the foundation for what's next: Part III of this book. We will delve into creating a daily routine that holistically improves your health by incorporating all the practices we've discussed so far—grounding, early morning sunshine, and deep breathing. Imagine a life where you wake up invigorated by the morning sun, ground yourself to release stress, and use deep breathing techniques to maintain a calm and focused mind throughout the day. Stay tuned to transform this vision into your reality.

CHAPTER 7: DESIGNING YOUR 10-MINUTE MORNING RITUAL

From Theory to Action: Crafting Your Personalized 10-Minute Morning Ritual for Holistic Well-Being

The journey from understanding the science behind grounding, early morning sunshine, and deep breathing to actually incorporating these elements into your daily life begins here. So far, we've delved deep into the theoretical aspects—how each of these practices scientifically contributes to various dimensions of your well-being. Now, it's time to transition from theory to practice.

A consistent morning routine holds the power to set the tone for the rest of your day. Just as a strong foundation is essential for building a sturdy house, a well-crafted morning ritual is vital for long-term well-being. Think of it as your daily dose of self-care, a 10-minute investment that yields manifold returns throughout the day and, ultimately, your life.

In this chapter, we will guide you through creating your personalized 10-minute morning ritual that synergistically combines grounding, early morning sunshine, and deep breathing. The objective is to provide you with a practical framework that not only enriches your life but also fits seamlessly into your schedule. Let's dive in.

How to Combine All Three Pillars

The Optimized Morning Routine: A 10-Minute Guide to Grounding, Sunlight, and Deep Breathing

Creating an effective morning routine that harnesses the power of grounding, sunlight, and deep breathing might initially seem like a daunting task. However, with a bit of planning, you can easily condense these powerful practices into a manageable 10-minute routine that sets the tone for a highly productive and mentally enriching day. Here's how to go about it:

Step 1: Grounding (3 Minutes)

Begin your morning by engaging in grounding—a practice that entails making direct contact with the Earth's surface. This could mean stepping barefoot onto the grass in your backyard or using an indoor grounding mat if you're limited by space or weather. Grounding for just three minutes can have a significant impact; it can help you reduce stress hormones, improve your mood, and set a peaceful foundation for the day ahead.

Step 2: Early Morning Sunshine (4 Minutes)

Next, transition to a spot where you can catch some morning sunlight. Four minutes of sunlight exposure can do wonders for your well-being. This brief interaction with natural light helps regulate your internal circadian clock, enhancing sleep quality, and boosting your mood through the release of serotonin. If you're doing the grounding in your yard, you can easily combine it with this step.

Step 3: Deep Breathing (3 Minutes)

To round off your morning ritual, spend the final three minutes on deep breathing exercises, such as the 4-7-8 technique. This focused breathing calms your nervous system, primes your lungs for optimal oxygen exchange, and sets a balanced emotional and cognitive baseline for the day ahead.

Time Allocation Overview

- **Grounding:** 3 minutes
- **Early Morning Sunshine:** 4 minutes
- **Deep Breathing:** 3 minutes

By intentionally weaving these practices into a concise 10-minute morning ritual, you create a synergistic effect that amplifies the benefits of each individual component. Not only does this make your morning routine more effective, but it also streamlines your efforts towards better overall well-being. This well-calibrated sequence allows you to start your day on a note of serenity and readiness, armed with the best tools nature offers for mental, emotional, and physical health.

The Power of Synergy: Amplified Benefits Through Combining Grounding, Early Morning Sunshine, and Deep Breathing

When practiced individually, grounding, early morning sunlight exposure, and deep breathing are all highly effective wellness strategies. However, when these elements are intentionally combined in a single routine, their benefits don't just add up—they multiply. Here's how these elements can synergistically enhance your well-being:

Grounding + Early Morning Sunshine: The Mood-Boosting Duo

Combining grounding with exposure to early morning sunlight can supercharge your mood more than either could alone. Sunlight is a natural catalyst for the production of serotonin, the "feel-good" hormone, which plays a critical role in elevating mood and promoting a sense of well-being. Grounding, on the other hand, has been shown to reduce inflammation and stress. When you ground yourself while basking in the morning sun, you amplify the mood-enhancing effects of both practices, offering a potent lift to your emotional state.

Grounding + Deep Breathing: The Stress-Busting Combination

Marrying the practice of grounding with deep breathing can take your stress management to the next level. Grounding alone has been scientifically shown to reduce inflammation, a key contributor to stress. Deep breathing, particularly techniques like the 4-7-8 method, induces relaxation by calming the nervous system. When you engage in deep breathing while grounded, you accentuate the anti-inflammatory and relaxation effects of both practices. The outcome? A remarkably effective stress-management strategy that relaxes both body and mind.

Early Morning Sunshine + Deep Breathing: The Energy-Enhancing Pair

Pairing early morning sunlight exposure with deep breathing exercises can significantly improve your metabolic rate and overall energy levels. Sunlight exposure has a well-documented role in enhancing metabolism, while deep breathing improves oxygen exchange in the lungs. When these two are practiced together, they synergize to optimize your energy levels and oxygenate your cells more efficiently.

In summary, combining these elements into a single routine creates a unique, synergistic effect that amplifies the individual benefits of each practice. Whether you're seeking a mood boost, stress reduction, or enhanced energy levels, integrating grounding, early morning sunshine, and deep breathing into a single regimen is a powerful way to elevate your wellness journey.

Personalization Tips

For Different Lifestyles

Adapting Your Wellness Routine for Night Shift Workers: Grounding, Sunlight, and Deep Breathing Tailored to Your Schedule

Working the night shift can disrupt natural circadian rhythms, making it a challenge to incorporate wellness practices that are often best performed during daylight hours. However, there are effective ways to adapt grounding, sunlight exposure, and deep breathing to suit a nocturnal lifestyle.

Grounding for the Night Owl

Grounding doesn't have to be limited to daylight hours. The Earth emits its beneficial energies around the clock, and you can tap into them whenever it's convenient for you. If you find that stepping outdoors isn't an option due to your schedule or living situation, consider using a grounding mat indoors. Place it under your feet while you're seated or standing, and you can enjoy the same calming, inflammation-reducing effects as you would with direct contact to the Earth.

Sunlight Exposure at Unconventional Hours

One of the challenges of working night shifts is the reduced exposure to natural light, which plays a vital role in regulating your internal body clock. To compensate, consider using a light therapy lamp that mimics the wavelengths of natural sunlight. Spending just a few minutes in front of a light therapy lamp when you wake up or right before you start your shift can help regulate your circadian rhythms, boost your mood, and improve your alertness. Make sure to choose a lamp that is specifically designed for light therapy to get the full benefits.

Deep Breathing: Timeless and Universal

The beauty of deep breathing exercises is that they're not bound by the clock. Whether it's the middle of the day or the middle of the night, the physiological benefits remain the same. Techniques like 4-7-8 breathing can be practiced to calm your nervous system and prepare you mentally for the work ahead. Deep breathing is an adaptable tool in your wellness arsenal that is as effective at 3 a.m. as it is at 3 p.m.

By making these adjustments, night shift workers can customize a wellness routine that accommodates their unique schedules while still providing the grounding, mood-enhancing, and stress-reducing benefits that these practices offer.

A Wellness Routine for Busy Parents: Sneaking in Grounding, Sunlight, and Deep Breathing Amidst the Morning Chaos

Balancing a hectic family life with self-care often feels like a juggling act for busy parents. But there's good news: wellness practices such as grounding, early morning sunshine, and deep breathing can still find a home in your packed schedule, without needing large chunks of time. Here's how:

Grounding While Parenting

Standing barefoot on natural, conductive surfaces like stone or hardwood floors can be an effective grounding practice. If you have such flooring in your kitchen, you can easily incorporate grounding into your morning routine. While the kids are occupied with their breakfast, take a few minutes to stand barefoot on the floor. Close your eyes for a moment if you can, and feel the Earth's energy as you prepare for the whirlwind day ahead. This not only connects you to the Earth's stabilizing energy but also gives you a mental 'reset' before stepping into your busy parent role.

Catching Some Rays with the Kids

Sunlight exposure in the morning can help regulate your internal body clock and boost your mood. As a parent, your morning is often consumed by getting the kids ready for school. Use this time to also focus on your own well-being by stepping outside for a few minutes, either while preparing them for the day or immediately after dropping them off. These short bursts of natural light can significantly lift your mood and increase your alertness, making the challenges of parenting a bit easier to navigate.

Breathing Exercises on the Go

As parents, the drive back home or to work after dropping off the kids at school can be the only 'alone time' you get all day. Utilize this window for some deep breathing exercises. Techniques such as 4-7-8 breathing or diaphragmatic breathing can serve as powerful tools for stress reduction and mental clarity. Practice these in your car to set a calm tone for the rest of your day.

By creatively incorporating these wellness practices into your existing routine, you can manage to be both a dedicated parent and a proponent of your own well-being. It's not only possible but also beneficial for you—and by extension, your family—to fit in these moments of grounding, sunlight exposure, and deep breathing.

Maximizing Wellness in Limited-Space Environments: Grounding, Sunlight, and Deep Breathing in Compact Living Spaces

Living or working in confined areas might seem like an obstacle to incorporating wellness practices such as grounding, sunlight exposure, and deep breathing into your routine. However, it's completely feasible to adapt these beneficial activities to your spatial circumstances. Here's a closer look at how you can do it:

Grounding in a Shoebox

While standing barefoot on natural ground is the ideal way to ground yourself, that's not always possible in a small apartment or office cubicle. The solution? Grounding mats. These devices mimic the Earth's natural electrical field and can be placed under your desk or even on your bed. Simply put your feet on the mat while working or relaxing to reap the grounding benefits. They're a perfect way to incorporate grounding into limited spaces without disrupting your day.

Sunlight Through a Windowpane

If stepping outside isn't feasible due to space limitations, the next best thing is to get close to a window that allows in natural light. Sunlight has several health benefits, including the regulation of circadian rhythms and mood enhancement. Stand or sit near a window for a few minutes in the morning, letting the natural light hit your face and skin. This can stimulate the production of mood-enhancing hormones and help to reset your internal clock, thus setting a positive tone for the day ahead.

Breathing Room in Tight Quarters

Deep breathing requires no external tools or large spaces; all you need is yourself. Whether you're in a cramped office or a small apartment, you can easily practice deep breathing exercises like diaphragmatic breathing or the 4-7-8 method. These practices help in stress reduction, improved focus, and better oxygenation of your body. It could be while you're working at your desk, cooking in your small kitchen, or even waiting for the elevator. Simply take a few moments to focus on your breath, and you'll notice an immediate impact on your well-being.

Adapting wellness practices for limited spaces might require a bit of creativity and flexibility, but it's far from impossible. In fact, these adjustments could make you more mindful of your daily routines, helping you get the most wellness bang for your buck, no matter the square footage.

For Different Health Goals

Specialized Techniques for Stress Reduction: Grounding, Sunlight, and Deep Breathing Tailored to Calm

The cumulative toll of daily stressors can have significant repercussions on our overall well-being. That's why it's essential to incorporate specialized practices into your routine that are specifically designed to mitigate stress. Here's how you can optimize grounding, sunlight exposure, and deep breathing to target stress reduction.

Mindful Grounding for Inner Calm

When grounding, the goal is to connect deeply with the Earth to balance out any physical or emotional disruptions you may be experiencing. In a stress-focused routine, engage in grounding practices that require your complete attention and mindfulness. This could involve not just standing on a grounding mat or grass but also closing your eyes, feeling the Earth's energy flow through your feet, and visualizing it moving up through your body. This deep level of awareness can facilitate a mental shift, helping you unplug from stressors and plug into the Earth's natural calming energy.

Serene Sunlight: Basking in Shaded Glow

Direct sunlight is potent and invigorating but might not be ideal when you're looking to reduce stress. Instead, find a serene, shaded spot where you can still experience natural daylight, but without the intensity. Whether it's under a tree or a shaded part of your porch, the key is to absorb indirect sunlight. This still helps in serotonin production—often referred to as the "happy hormone"—but without overstimulating your senses, allowing you to feel calm and centered.

Breathwork for Stress Relief: The 4-7-8 Technique

Breathing exercises are versatile, offering benefits that range from increased focus to energy enhancement. However, when dealing with stress, it's helpful to focus on techniques specifically designed to induce a state of relaxation. The 4-7-8 method involves inhaling through the nose for 4 seconds, holding the breath for 7 seconds, and then exhaling fully through the mouth for 8 seconds. This exercise slows down your breathing rate and calms your nervous system, making it an effective stress-relieving technique.

By incorporating these specialized grounding, sunlight, and deep breathing techniques into your daily routine, you're not just going through the motions of self-care—you're strategically tackling stress. These tailored activities aim to counteract stress at its core, offering a holistic and effective approach to maintaining your emotional equilibrium.

Optimizing Sleep Through Grounding, Sunlight, and Breathwork: A Tailored Evening and Morning Routine

While most wellness routines target general well-being, you can focus on optimizing specific outcomes, such as sleep improvement, by tailoring your activities. Here's how you can adjust grounding, sunlight exposure, and deep breathing techniques to enhance your sleep quality.

Grounding for Restful Nights: The Pre-Sleep Session

While grounding is often considered a daytime activity, incorporating it into your evening routine can pave the way for better sleep. Studies indicate that grounding can improve sleep quality by regulating cortisol levels and reducing inflammation. To tailor this practice for sleep improvement, engage in a short grounding session before bedtime. Spend a few minutes standing or sitting with your feet touching natural surfaces, such as grass or a grounding mat. This evening grounding session can help you unwind and prepare your body for restful, uninterrupted sleep.

Sunlight to Regulate Circadian Rhythm: Timing is Key

It may seem counterintuitive, but morning sunlight can have a profound impact on your ability to fall asleep later in the evening. Exposure to natural light in the morning helps regulate your internal body clock, also known as your circadian rhythm. This, in turn, aids in the production of melatonin—the sleep hormone—in the evening, helping you fall asleep at the appropriate time. Make it a point to spend a few minutes outside in the morning, even if it's just during a quick walk or while sipping your morning coffee on the patio.

Deep Breathing for Relaxation: Diaphragmatic Breathing

The quality of your sleep is not solely determined by what you do just before bedtime but is also influenced by your activities throughout the day. Integrating diaphragmatic breathing into your morning routine can set the stage for a better night's sleep. This deep breathing technique involves breathing deeply into your diaphragm rather than shallowly into your chest, promoting overall relaxation. As you go through your day, this relaxed state can help mitigate stress, which often interferes with sleep, ensuring that you're better prepared for a good night's rest when the time comes.

By specifically tailoring each of these practices—grounding, sunlight exposure, and deep breathing—you're taking a targeted approach to sleep improvement. The benefits of better sleep ripple outward, affecting everything from your mood and stress levels to your cognitive function and overall health.

Unlocking Cognitive Power: Tailored Grounding, Sunlight, and Breathwork Techniques for Mental Clarity

Achieving optimal cognitive function is an aspiration for many, especially in today's fast-paced and mentally demanding world. Grounding, sunlight exposure, and deep breathing—often promoted for general well-being—can also be highly effective tools for cognitive enhancement when tailored to this specific goal. Here's how:

Focused Grounding: Setting the Stage for Mental Acuity

Grounding has been traditionally associated with emotional and physical well-being, but it also offers benefits for mental clarity. By physically connecting with the Earth, you can induce a state of mindfulness that helps clear mental fog and distractions. For cognitive enhancement, a brief, focused grounding session can be extremely effective. During these moments, direct your thoughts inward and attempt to clear your mind of clutter. Whether you choose to connect with the Earth by standing barefoot on grass or using a grounding mat, the aim is to create a mental landscape that sets the stage for enhanced cognitive function.

Sunlight for Alertness: The Cognitive Boost You Didn't Know You Needed

Research indicates that exposure to natural sunlight can significantly improve alertness and cognitive performance. Sunlight triggers the release of serotonin, often termed the "happy hormone," but it's also essential for mood regulation and mental alertness. A few minutes of morning sunlight can set a positive tone for the day and improve your cognitive abilities. If you work indoors, make an effort to take short breaks to step outside or work by a window to harness this natural cognitive enhancer.

Breathwork for Concentration: Box Breathing Technique

Deep breathing exercises are known to reduce stress and improve physiological function, but they can also be tailored for cognitive improvement. Specifically, the box breathing technique can be an excellent tool for enhancing focus and concentration. This method involves inhaling, holding the breath, exhaling, and then holding the breath again, all for equal counts (usually four seconds). Practicing box breathing helps to optimize oxygen flow to the brain and provides a momentary pause to refresh your mental state, making it an ideal technique for tasks requiring intense focus.

By deliberately adapting grounding, sunlight, and deep breathing techniques for cognitive enhancement, you're not just improving your general well-being but also optimizing your brain's performance. With consistent practice, these tailored activities can become a powerful regimen for boosting your mental acuity.

These modifications ensure that you're not following a one-size-fits-all approach but tailoring your morning routine to meet your specific lifestyle and health goals.

CONCLUSION

In this chapter, we've journeyed from the theoretical to the practical, laying out comprehensive ways to blend the three powerful pillars of wellbeing—grounding, early morning sunshine, and deep breathing—into a quick, effective 10-minute morning ritual. From suggestions on the ideal sequence to tips on personalizing the routine for different lifestyles and health goals, you now have the tools you need to embark on a transformative journey toward long-term well-being.

But knowing is just the first step; application is what truly counts. That's why the next chapter introduces a 30-Day Challenge designed to make your new morning routine a sustainable habit. The challenge will provide daily guidance and actionable steps to help you implement and stick to your personalized ritual, setting you on the path for a lifetime of improved health and happiness. Stay tuned, the journey to holistic wellness is just beginning.

CHAPTER 8: THE 30-DAY CHALLENGE

EMBARKING ON THE 30-DAY CHALLENGE: YOUR BLUEPRINT FOR SUSTAINABLE WELLNESS AND HABIT MASTERY

The journey to lasting health and well-being is not a sprint but a marathon, and the key to long-term success lies in consistency and habit formation. Scientific research consistently underscores the power of habits in shaping our lives, influencing everything from our daily routines to our long-term health outcomes. This is why we've designed the 30-Day Challenge—a structured yet flexible blueprint aimed to guide you in ingraining these life-enhancing practices into your daily routine.

So, what does this challenge entail? Over the next month, you will be guided week-by-week through a carefully designed program that incorporates grounding, early morning sunshine, and deep breathing. We'll start by establishing the basics, then move to refinement and personalization, deepen the practice, and finally reach mastery. Alongside this, we will focus on tracking your progress and using data to further personalize your experience.

By the end of the 30 days, you won't just have a powerful morning routine; you'll have a sustainable practice that contributes to your overall health and wellness for years to come. Let's get started!

WEEK BY WEEK GUIDE

WEEK 1: LAYING THE FOUNDATIONS OF YOUR MORNING ROUTINE FOR LASTING TRANSFORMATION

In the first week, your journey begins with the basics—understanding and incorporating three pillars of well-being into your daily routine:

grounding, early morning sunshine, and deep breathing. The aim of this introductory week is to make these practices second nature, setting the stage for more personalized and advanced techniques in the weeks to come.

Grounding: Your Earthly Connection for Well-Being

Your first task is to spend at least 2 minutes daily grounding yourself. Grounding, or earthing, involves making direct contact with the Earth, typically by walking barefoot on natural surfaces like grass, soil, or sand. This practice is believed to neutralize free radicals in your body and offer a plethora of other health benefits. If going outside is not feasible, you can also use grounding mats designed to simulate the Earth's electromagnetic fields. At the end of the week, you should feel more comfortable with the practice and start to notice subtle shifts in your mood or physical state.

Early Morning Sunshine: The All-Natural Mood Lifter

Your next task is to immerse yourself in early morning sunshine for another 2 minutes per day. Exposure to natural light, especially in the morning, helps regulate your circadian rhythms, boosts your mood by triggering the release of serotonin, and offers several other health benefits. Weather permitting, step outside and stand or sit in a comfortable position where you can soak up the rays. The aim is to make this a regular part of your routine, preparing you for further refinements in Week 2.

Deep Breathing: Calmness in Every Breath

The final basic pillar is deep breathing. Dedicate another 2 minutes of your day to practice the 4-7-8 breathing technique: inhale through the nose for 4 seconds, hold the breath for 7 seconds, and exhale through the mouth for 8 seconds. This simple yet effective practice can reduce stress, improve your focus, and enhance your respiratory system. It acts as a mental reset button and can be done virtually anywhere, making it a versatile addition to your wellness toolkit.

Summary of Week 1 Goals and Daily Tasks:

- **Grounding**: Spend at least 2 minutes walking barefoot on natural surfaces like grass, or use a grounding mat.
- **Early Morning Sunshine**: Dedicate 2 minutes to stand or sit outdoors to absorb natural light.
- **Deep Breathing**: Invest another 2 minutes in practicing the 4-7-8 breathing pattern.

By adhering to these foundational practices, you're not just ticking off a checklist but laying the groundwork for a transformative morning routine. Week 1 is crucial as it sets the tone for the rest of your journey, helping you get comfortable with these core practices and readying you for the refinement and personalization stages ahead.

Week 2: Fine-Tuning Your Morning Ritual for a Custom Fit

As you enter the second week of your transformative journey, it's time to take stock. Reflect on your experiences from Week 1 and assess how you've been feeling physically and emotionally. The purpose of this week is to refine and personalize your approach, making subtle adjustments to tailor each pillar—grounding, early morning sunshine, and deep breathing—to better align with your lifestyle and needs.

Grounding: Expanding Your Earthen Palette

In Week 1, you established the practice of grounding for at least 2 minutes per day. Now, let's refine it. Consider varying the terrains you walk on—perhaps venture from grass to sand or soil. Each type of terrain offers unique benefits. Experimenting with different times of day could also help you discover when grounding has the most potent effects for you. Whether you're an early bird or a night owl, tuning into your body's natural rhythms can amplify the benefits you reap from this practice.

Sun Exposure: Beyond the Basics

Having soaked up 2 minutes of early morning sunshine daily, now you're ready to tweak the parameters. Maybe you're a person who benefits from longer exposure to the sun. Try extending the duration and observe how your body reacts. Alternatively, try different positions; sitting versus standing can offer varied experiences. Be sure to listen to your body, though; excessive sun exposure can be harmful.

Deep Breathing: Adding a New Dimension

Deep breathing is more than just a stress reliever; it's a versatile tool that can be adapted to meet various needs. If you've been using the 4-7-8 method, consider switching to a different technique like box breathing. In box breathing, you inhale, hold, exhale, and hold again, all for equal time counts, usually starting at four seconds. This is a fantastic way to further enhance your focus and keep your stress levels in check.

Summary of Week 2 Goals and Daily Tasks:

- **Grounding**: Experiment with walking on different natural surfaces or try grounding at varied times of the day.
- **Sun Exposure**: Personalize your routine by tweaking the duration or changing your physical position during sun exposure.
- **Deep Breathing**: Introduce a new breathing technique to your practice, such as box breathing.

Week 2 is all about ownership. You're not just following a preset plan; you're actively involved in molding it to suit your unique constitution. By the end of this week, each practice should start feeling less like a daily task and more like a personal ritual, bringing you closer to mastering a morning routine that truly resonates with you.

Week 3: Amplifying Your Morning Ritual for Potent Benefits

As you transition into the third week of your journey, the focus shifts from simply practicing to mastering your daily rituals. By now, you have a foundational grasp of each of the three pillars: grounding, early morning sunshine, and deep breathing. Week 3 invites you to amplify the potency of each practice by adding nuanced layers of complexity, thereby making them more effective and resonant for you.

Grounding: From Connection to Communion

During this week, aim to spend at least 3 minutes grounding each day, extending your initial 2-minute sessions. Use this extra time to deepen your awareness and connection to the Earth. You might find it helpful to close your eyes for a moment, feeling the natural terrain underfoot as an extension of your own body. This mindful approach can help transform your grounding practice from a simple physical connection to a more profound emotional and spiritual communion with the Earth.

Sun Exposure: Vitality Through Movement

By now, you're accustomed to spending a couple of minutes soaking up the morning sun. This week, incorporate some light stretches or body movements as you bathe in the sun's rays. Simple activities like arm circles, toe touches, or neck rolls can awaken your body while helping you absorb Vitamin D more effectively. The act of coupling sun exposure with physical movement creates a synergistic effect that enlivens both body and mind.

Deep Breathing: The Breath as an Anchor

As you've grown comfortable with basic and alternative breathing techniques, now aim to deepen your practice. Incorporate mindfulness techniques by focusing entirely on your breath. Visualize the air flowing in and out of your lungs, and pay attention to the sensation of breath entering and leaving your nostrils. This mindfulness layer not only deepens your relaxation but also enhances your awareness and presence.

Summary of Week 3 Goals and Daily Tasks:

- **Grounding**: Extend your time spent grounding to at least 3 minutes, deepening your connection with Earth.
- **Sun Exposure**: Add light stretching or simple body movements to your sun-soaking ritual.
- **Deep Breathing**: Incorporate mindfulness into your breathing practice, focusing purely on your breath.

Tips for Overcoming Obstacles:

- **Weather Constraints**: If you can't practice grounding or sun exposure due to poor weather, consider indoor alternatives like grounding mats or light therapy lamps.
- **Mind Wandering During Deep Breathing**: If you notice your mind drifting away, gently guide your focus back to your breath. Consider using a simple mantra to maintain focus.

By adding these layers to your practice, Week 3 serves as a powerful bridge leading you towards mastery. Your morning routine should now be starting to feel like a truly holistic wellness ritual, designed uniquely for you.

Week 4: Culminating Your Morning Rituals for Lifelong Mastery and Well-Being

The journey you embarked on four weeks ago reaches its climactic stage in Week 4. By now, each element of your morning routine—grounding, absorbing early morning sunshine, and deep breathing—should be comfortably integrated into your daily life. The final week is all about taking this familiarity to the realm of mastery.

It's time to finalize, refine, and commit to these practices as lifelong habits.

Grounding: The Pinnacle of Earthly Connection

Having explored various aspects of grounding in the past weeks, you now have a good idea of what works best for you. Consistently aim to spend at least 3 minutes grounding each day, choosing methods and terrains that have shown to be most effective and fulfilling for you. This could mean focusing on specific natural settings that you've found particularly rejuvenating or opting for a particular kind of grounding mat if you're indoors.

Sun Exposure: Setting the Gold Standard

With a few weeks of experimentation behind you, it's time to finalize your sun exposure routine. Whether it's spending 5 minutes in direct sunlight or incorporating stretches during this time, choose the activities and duration that have yielded the most noticeable benefits. Make these practices your gold standard, setting the tone for how you engage with sunlight moving forward.

Deep Breathing: Perfecting the Art of Breath

Of all the breathing techniques you've tried, stick to the one that has resonated with you the most. Whether it's the 4-7-8 pattern or box breathing, make this technique your go-to method. Mastering this technique involves not just performing it correctly, but doing so with a degree of consciousness and intent that makes it second nature.

Preparing for the Future: Sustaining Your Practice

As you close this four-week chapter, look ahead to sustaining these practices for the long term:

- **Setting Reminders**: Use your smartphone or smart home devices to set daily reminders, ensuring that you never skip your routine.

- **Tracking Progress**: Consider using tracking apps or a dedicated journal to record your experiences, helping you refine your practices further over time.
- **Reflection and Commitment**: Take a moment to reflect on the transformative journey you've undertaken. Commit to making these practices a non-negotiable part of your life, recognizing their contribution to your overall well-being.

Summary of Week 4 Goals and Daily Tasks:

- **Grounding**: Master your grounding practice by consistently spending at least 3 minutes using the most effective methods.
- **Sun Exposure**: Finalize your sun exposure routine based on what you've found most beneficial.
- **Deep Breathing**: Master your chosen breathing technique.

By the end of Week 4, these practices should not just be tasks but meaningful rituals. You are not merely performing these activities; you are embodying them, letting them enrich your life in myriad ways. Congratulations, you're now well on your way to a lifelong journey of wellness and self-discovery.

Tracking Progress

Journaling and Documentation: Your Personal Compass for Navigating the 30-Day Challenge

The act of journaling serves as a two-fold tool in your transformative journey. First, it offers a structured framework for you to objectively measure your progress across the various pillars of grounding, sun exposure, and deep breathing. Second, it acts as a reflective space for you to record your subjective experiences, providing invaluable feedback that can be used to refine and personalize your routine. As you embark on or continue with your 30-day challenge, understanding how to make the most of your journal can be a game-changer.

Suggested Journal Prompts: Navigating Your Inner Landscape

Journaling about your feelings and experiences is akin to having a conversation with yourself. Below are some journal prompts to guide this internal dialogue:

- **How did each pillar make you feel today?** Describe any physical or emotional sensations. Did grounding make you feel calm? Did the morning sunlight elevate your mood?
- **Were there any challenges or obstacles? How did you overcome them?** Perhaps it rained, and you couldn't ground outside. How did you adapt? Did you use a grounding mat? Did you move to a different location to catch some sun?
- **What specific benefits or changes did you notice in your mood, energy levels, or mental clarity?** Were you more focused during the day? Did you notice you were less irritable?

Key Metrics to Record: The Pulse of Your Progress

Journaling is not just about qualitative insights; it's equally important to note quantifiable metrics to measure your journey's success objectively.

- **Duration Spent on Each Pillar**: Record the exact time spent grounding, absorbing sun, and deep breathing. This will help you track how consistent you are and if you're meeting your daily goals.
- **Quality of Sleep (Scale of 1-10)**: Use this scale to rate your sleep each night. Look for patterns over time. Are you consistently scoring higher as you progress through the challenge?

- **Mood or Stress Level (Scale of 1-10)**: Rate your emotional state at different times during the day to gauge the effectiveness of your routine.
- **Cognitive Performance**: If measurable, make note of how long you can focus without interruption or the rate at which you are completing tasks. This can help you gauge the impact of your routine on mental functions.

By diligently journaling both qualitative and quantitative aspects of your experience, you're essentially setting up a feedback loop. This enables you to continuously assess, adapt, and perfect your routine, giving you the most holistic view of how this transformative 30-Day Challenge is reshaping your mornings and, by extension, your life.

Data and Feedback: The Objective Lens to Fine-Tune Your 30-Day Challenge

While journaling offers a personalized, introspective look into your journey, objective tools such as sleep trackers, mood apps, and spreadsheets offer the complementary advantage of unbiased, quantifiable metrics. The amalgamation of both subjective and objective data provides a comprehensive, 360-degree view that can significantly augment your understanding of your progress. Here's how you can harness these tools to optimize your 30-Day Challenge experience.

Measuring Progress: Tools of the Trade

1. **Sleep Trackers**: These wearables or smartphone apps can give you detailed insights into the quality and duration of your sleep. They often capture data on sleep cycles, restlessness, and sometimes even heart rate and oxygen levels.
2. **Mood Apps**: These mobile applications allow you to record your emotional state at different points throughout the day. Over

time, the data compiles into patterns that can help you understand mood fluctuations and their possible triggers.

3. **Spreadsheets**: Sometimes, the simplest tools are the most effective. A basic spreadsheet can serve as an all-in-one dashboard where you can log key quantitative metrics like time spent on each pillar, sleep duration, and mood scores.

INTERPRETING YOUR DATA: THE ART OF FINE-TUNING

- **Look for Patterns or Trends**: Over the course of the 30-Day Challenge, you'll start to notice patterns in your data. Are you gradually sleeping better as the weeks pass? Is your mood more stable? These are the kinds of questions your data can help you answer.

- **Make Informed Adjustments**: Having hard data allows you to adapt your routine with precision. If your sleep quality has improved but your mood remains unchanged, this could indicate that you may need to allocate more time or effort into your deep breathing exercises, for instance.

By skillfully combining the self-reflection of journaling with the empirical evidence provided by objective tools, you establish a robust feedback loop. This dual approach not only validates your efforts but also provides you with actionable insights to continually refine your routine. In essence, it equips you with the data-driven intelligence you need to make your 30-Day Challenge as effective and transformative as possible.

CONCLUSION

Congratulations on navigating through the 30-Day Challenge! This journey was designed to equip you with the tools and techniques for incorporating the three pillars—grounding, early morning sunshine, and deep breathing—into your daily life. The importance of consistency and habit formation can't be stressed enough; it's the ongoing practice that yields long-term health benefits.

As you've learned, each of these pillars contributes to your overall well-being in unique ways, from enhancing your mood and cognitive function to improving your sleep and stress levels. And remember, this is just the beginning. The true value of this practice lies in making it a permanent part of your daily routine.

A Call to Action

We encourage you to make these practices a lifelong commitment. The beauty of this routine is its simplicity and adaptability. As your life changes, so too can your 10-minute morning ritual. Continue to track your progress, adapt the routine to meet new challenges or goals, and above all, invest in yourself each and every day.

By committing to this practice long-term, you're setting the stage for a healthier, happier, and more fulfilling life. And isn't that the ultimate goal? So go ahead, take the pledge to continue this enriching routine and be amazed at the ongoing transformation it brings to your life.

CHAPTER 9: OVERCOMING COMMON OBSTACLES

Strategies for Keeping Your 10-Minute Morning Ritual Unshakeable

Let's be honest, life is unpredictable. Despite your best intentions, there will be days when sticking to your 10-minute morning ritual feels like an uphill battle. Perhaps it's inclement weather, a demanding work schedule, or unexpected family commitments that throw a wrench into your plans. It's important to acknowledge that these challenges are a normal part of life and don't make you any less committed to your well-being.

The goal of this chapter is straightforward yet vital: to arm you with practical solutions for overcoming common obstacles. Whether you're dealing with seasonal changes that make grounding more difficult or navigating a hectic daily schedule that seemingly leaves no room for self-care, this chapter has got you covered. By the end of it, you'll be well-prepared to make your 10-minute morning ritual a resilient and sustainable practice, come rain or shine, busy days or lazy weekends.

Weather Conditions

Adapting to Seasonal Changes: Weather-Proof Your 10-Minute Morning Routine

Seasonal changes offer more than just a shift in weather; they provide a window of opportunity to reinvigorate and adapt your daily practices. Whether it's the chilling winds of winter or the scorching heat of summer, here's how you can seamlessly transition your routine to suit the season's unique demands.

Embracing the Cold: Winter Adaptations

1. **Indoor Grounding**: If the cold weather discourages you from stepping outside, don't fret. Grounding mats can replicate the

effects of connecting with the Earth right in the comfort of your home. You can also get creative and touch grounded objects like radiators or even bare metal plumbing for a few minutes to achieve a similar effect.

2. **Utilize Natural Light**: Sunshine can be sparse during the winter months, but it's still there. Position yourself near a window during sunrise, and let the early rays filter in as you practice your deep breathing exercises. The natural light, although diminished, still carries beneficial properties.

NAVIGATING THE HEAT: SUMMER ADAPTATIONS

1. **Shaded Grounding**: High temperatures shouldn't deter you from grounding. Look for areas with ample shade, like a tree canopy or an outdoor structure. Alternatively, ground during the cooler hours of early morning or late evening when the sun's intensity is reduced.

2. **Indirect Sun Exposure**: When the sun blazes too strongly for direct exposure, adapt your routine. Use light-blocking curtains to soften the sunlight, positioning yourself to still receive indirect natural light during your morning practices.

By paying attention to these seasonal nuances and adapting accordingly, you maintain the integrity of your 10-minute morning routine while embracing the creativity that comes with change. This flexibility ensures that your daily practices remain resilient, effective, and enjoyable, regardless of what Mother Nature has to offer.

WEATHER-PROOFING YOUR ROUTINE: EQUIP, ADAPT, AND THRIVE THROUGH SEASONS

Being fully prepared for various weather conditions is the key to making your routine durable and resilient. No matter the season or the elements you face, a well-thought-out approach to weather-proofing ensures that your 10-minute morning ritual remains a steadfast part of your day. Here's how you can equip yourself and make quick adjustments to adapt to any climate.

Smart Investment in Equipment and Clothing

1. **Moisture-Wicking Apparel**: For the hot and humid months, invest in moisture-wicking clothing. These fabrics draw sweat away from your body, helping you to feel cooler and more comfortable during your morning grounding and sun exposure routines.

2. **Warm, Breathable Layers**: For cold climates, a few warm but breathable layers can make all the difference. Insulated clothing keeps you warm without causing overheating, allowing you to comfortably step outside for your morning practices.

3. **All-Weather Outdoor Mat**: Don't underestimate the power of a good mat. An all-weather outdoor mat designed specifically for grounding can handle mud, rain, and snow while still providing an effective connection to the Earth. Plus, these mats are typically easy to clean and quick to dry.

Quick Adjustments for Instant Adaptability

1. **Indoor Grounding Solutions**: Sometimes stepping outdoors isn't practical or comfortable. In such cases, a grounding mat or a conductive wristband serves as a quick indoor alternative. Keeping these tools on hand ensures you never miss a day of grounding.

2. **UV Lamps for Simulated Sunlight**: Sunshine is sparse during the winter months, but that shouldn't deprive you of its benefits. UV lamps designed to mimic natural sunlight can be used in small doses during your deep breathing exercises. They provide a temporary substitute, offering some of the mood-boosting and vitamin-generating advantages of actual sunlight.

By strategically investing in equipment and being prepared to make on-the-spot adjustments, you construct a routine that's not just weather-resistant but weather-proof. These preparations give you the flexibility to adapt without disrupting the core benefits of your 10-minute morning ritual. Regardless of what Mother Nature decides to do, you'll be well-equipped to maintain your practice consistently and effectively.

Time Management

Conquering Busy Schedules: Fitting Wellness into Your Day No Matter How Packed Your Agenda

Life's relentless pace can often make even a 10-minute morning routine feel like a luxury. However, the very essence of a packed schedule screams for the need for self-care and well-being. Here's how to fit your 10-minute morning routine into a busy day without sacrificing its benefits.

Strategically Using Transitional Moments

1. **The Wake-Up Window**: The moments just after you wake up are often spent reaching for your phone or contemplating the day ahead. Instead, immediately start with your 3-minute grounding routine to maximize this transitional moment. You're already transitioning from sleep to wakefulness; make this time doubly effective by incorporating grounding.

2. **Pre-Shower Pause**: Many people have a few minutes of downtime before stepping into the shower. Use this moment to practice your deep breathing for 4 minutes. It's a quiet time where you're less likely to be interrupted and can focus entirely on your breathing.

Leveraging Technology for Reminders

1. **Set Daily Alarms**: Use your smartphone to set a recurring daily alarm specifically labeled for your 10-minute routine. Having a dedicated alarm, distinct from your regular wake-up alarm, serves as a specialized cue that's hard to ignore.

2. **Calendar Alerts**: Take it a step further by creating a calendar event for your routine, complete with reminders. It will pop up on your devices, serving as another nudge and adding an extra layer of accountability.

Breaking It Down: The Piecemeal Approach

If setting aside a full 10 minutes at once is absolutely unfeasible, consider breaking the routine into smaller parts:

1. **Morning Grounding**: Spend 3 minutes on grounding as soon as you wake up.

2. **Mid-Morning Breathing**: Dedicate a 4-minute block for deep breathing during your mid-morning break.

3. **Late Morning Sunshine**: Finally, reserve 3 minutes for soaking in some sunlight later in the morning. Even this piecemeal approach can give you cumulative benefits when consistently followed.

By being strategic with your transitional moments, leveraging technology for reminders, and having the flexibility to break down the routine, you can seamlessly embed wellness into your busy life. It's all about being agile with your self-care practices, just as you would be in tackling the demands of a hectic schedule. Remember, a busy life needs a balanced you, and these strategies will ensure you find that balance.

The Cornerstones of Routine Success: Prioritization and Consistency in Your Wellness Journey

When life gets chaotic, maintaining a wellness routine can feel like one more task on an already overflowing to-do list. However, your health is the one thing that should never be compromised. Here's how to keep your wellness regimen a priority and maintain consistency, even amidst the chaos of life.

Making Wellness Non-Negotiable: The Sacred Blocks

1. **Calendar Blocking**: Reserve a specific time slot in your calendar, just as you would for a crucial business meeting or a doctor's appointment. This act elevates your routine from an optional task to a committed appointment. Color-code this block, set reminders, and treat this time as sacred—absolutely non-negotiable.

2. **Visible Cues**: Place your grounding mat, deep-breathing props, or any other tools essential for your routine in conspicuous spots. The more visible these items are, the more likely they'll serve as a constant, gentle nudge towards your health commitment.

Navigating Life's Curveballs: Staying Committed Amidst Interruptions

1. **Revisiting Your 'Why'**: In those moments when you feel like giving up or skipping a day, revisit your initial motivations for starting this routine. Whether it's improved mental clarity, enhanced physical health, or better stress management, reminding yourself of your 'why' can reignite your commitment.

2. **Don't Aim for Perfection**: Perfectionism is the enemy of progress. If you miss a day, it's easy to fall into the trap of thinking you've failed and should abandon the effort altogether. Avoid this pitfall. Simply pick up where you left off. In the

grand scheme, a day or two doesn't detract from the long-term benefits you're accruing.

By employing thoughtful prioritization strategies and fostering a commitment to consistency, you transform your 10-minute morning ritual from a luxury into a staple of your daily life. This makes your routine resilient, able to withstand whatever twists and turns life may throw your way. So, block the time, set the cues, reignite your motivations, and keep going—your future self will thank you for it.

CONCLUSION

In this chapter, we've navigated through some of the most common roadblocks that could disrupt your 10-minute morning routine. From adapting to seasonal changes and weather-proofing your ritual, to time management strategies for busy schedules and conflicting commitments, the aim has been to provide you with a toolkit of solutions to stay on course.

At the core of maintaining this ritual lies the importance of flexibility and adaptability. Your routine is not a rigid set of rules, but rather a flexible guideline that serves your well-being. Whether you're facing a snowstorm or a jam-packed calendar, remember that the essence of this practice is to enhance your health and life. Adaptability is not a departure from the routine; it's an integral part of it.

By adopting a flexible approach, you not only make your 10-minute morning ritual resilient to challenges but also ensure that it evolves along with you, making it a sustainable, long-term commitment for ongoing health benefits.

CHAPTER 10: ADVANCED TIPS AND HACKS

Elevate Your Morning: Advanced Tips to Supercharge Your 10-Minute Ritual

Having spent the previous chapters focusing on the foundational elements of your 10-minute morning routine and overcoming potential obstacles, it's time to shift gears. We are moving from merely sustaining your practice to optimizing it for maximum efficacy and enjoyment.

This final chapter will introduce you to a selection of advanced tips and hacks that can take your daily routine to the next level. From the convenience of grounding footwear to the hidden gems for capturing the most nourishing morning sunshine, get ready to up the ante on your 10-minute morning ritual. Your commitment to a healthier life doesn't have to stop at the basics. There's a world of enhancements waiting to make your mornings even more beneficial. Let's dive in.

Grounding Footwear

Going Beyond Barefoot: The Multifaceted Advantages of Grounding Footwear

There's something innately calming and invigorating about the sensation of your bare feet touching the earth. However, while the idea of walking barefoot might evoke a sense of freedom and connection to nature, it's not always feasible in our modern lifestyles. Whether it's the hustle and bustle of city living or the rugged terrain of a hiking trail, various factors can make grounding a challenging endeavor. This is where grounding footwear comes to your rescue, offering a practical, versatile, and efficient alternative.

Bridging Nature and Practicality: The Core Benefits

1. **Electron Transfer**: One of the most significant benefits of grounding footwear is its ability to mimic the electron transfer you'd get from walking barefoot. Through conductive materials, these specialized shoes maintain your electrical connection to the Earth, offering the same physiological benefits like reduced inflammation and improved sleep quality.

2. **Safety and Protection**: While natural terrain might be inviting, it can also be unpredictable. Sharp stones, thorny bushes, or even fragments of glass can pose risks to your feet. Grounding shoes protect against such potential hazards, offering the dual benefits of grounding and physical protection.

3. **Versatility in Daily Life**: With grounding shoes, you're not restricted to specific settings or activities. Whether it's a brisk walk in an urban park or an adventurous hike in the wilderness, grounding footwear adapts to your lifestyle needs. The convenience makes them an excellent addition to your daily routine, extending the benefits of grounding beyond your dedicated morning ritual.

A Glimpse into Popular Options

1. **Earthing Shoes**: These are the all-rounders of grounding footwear. Known for their comfort and efficacy, they're a hit among people who want grounding to be a seamless part of their everyday life.

2. **Grounding Sandals**: If you're residing in or visiting a warmer climate, grounding sandals offer a more open and airy alternative, allowing your feet to breathe while still enjoying the benefits of grounding.

3. **Grounding Boots**: For the adventurers who are drawn to the more rugged terrains, grounding boots provide an ideal solution. These boots offer the sturdiness required for

challenging trails without compromising on the grounding effect.

By embracing grounding footwear, you manage to sustain your grounding practice in a practical, safe, and flexible manner. This adds a layer of versatility to your wellness regimen, allowing you to incorporate the benefits of grounding into various facets of your life. With the right pair, you're not just walking; you're walking towards a healthier, more balanced life.

The Art of Making an Informed Choice: How to Select the Perfect Grounding Footwear

Choosing the right pair of grounding footwear is a critical decision that has a far-reaching impact on your daily routine and overall well-being. As the saying goes, "You're going to walk a mile in these shoes," so you want to make sure those miles contribute positively to your health. The selection process involves several key considerations, each contributing to the overall efficacy and convenience of your grounding experience.

Key Criteria for Selection

1. **Material Matters**: The foundational aspect of grounding footwear is the conductive material used in its construction. Options like leather and specialized conductive rubber facilitate the crucial electron transfer between your body and the Earth. These materials not only make grounding possible but also maintain the flow of natural energy to enhance the overall experience.

2. **Comfort Is Key**: If your shoes are uncomfortable, the chances are high that they'll end up collecting dust in your closet. Comfort is essential for any footwear but especially so for grounding shoes that you might be wearing for extended periods. Look for designs that provide good arch support, breathable material, and

an overall snug fit. The comfort level should be such that it encourages frequent use, thereby maximizing the benefits you derive from grounding.

3. **Built to Last**: Quality grounding shoes are more than a purchase; they're an investment in your well-being. This makes durability a vital criterion. Consider factors like stitching quality, material resilience, and overall craftsmanship. A well-made pair of grounding shoes can withstand the wear and tear of daily use and diverse terrains, offering you value in the long run.

CONSULT THE WISDOM OF THE CROWD AND THE EXPERTS

1. **User Reviews**: These are your go-to for real-world insights into how the shoes perform. Platforms like online marketplaces and wellness-focused forums often host user reviews that cover aspects ranging from comfort to durability. Look for consistent patterns in reviews to gauge the product's strengths and weaknesses.

2. **Expert Opinions**: Experts in the grounding and wellness industry often publish reviews or recommendations that dig deep into the scientific and practical aspects of grounding footwear. Blogs, articles, and videos from trusted sources can provide a more nuanced understanding, aiding you in making an educated choice.

By meticulously considering these aspects and leveraging both user reviews and expert insights, you set the stage for an informed decision. Remember, the right pair of grounding footwear is not just an accessory but an integral component of your optimized morning routine. Choose wisely, and let every step you take be a step toward enhanced well-being.

Best Locations for Morning Sunshine

Urban vs. Natural Settings: Maximizing the Quality of Your Morning Sunshine Experience

In the quest for that perfect dose of morning sunshine to start your day right, the location can make a world of difference. Both urban and natural settings come with their unique sets of challenges and advantages, making it crucial to understand how each impacts your daily sunshine ritual.

Navigating the Urban Jungle for Sunshine

Urban settings often present a myriad of obstacles when it comes to soaking up the morning sun. Skyscrapers can cast long shadows, pollution may dull the sunshine, and green spaces are sometimes few and far between. However, there are clever ways to circumvent these challenges:

1. **Rise Above with Rooftops**: If you have access to a rooftop, it can be your private sanctuary for unobstructed morning sunshine. The higher elevation minimizes the influence of pollution and offers a direct line of sight to the sky.

2. **Park Life**: Local parks often serve as the lungs of a city and can be your go-to for cleaner air and brighter sunlight. Usually free from tall structures, these areas let you enjoy a decent amount of sunlight filtering through the trees.

3. **Window of Opportunity**: If stepping out isn't an option, consider utilizing large, east-facing windows. Opening the windows not only lets in the sunshine but also helps in air circulation, making the experience more wholesome.

Embracing Nature's Bounty

When it comes to the quality of sunshine, nothing compares to what natural settings have to offer. The air is cleaner, the sun is brighter, and the experience is more tranquil.

1. **Coastal Bliss**: Beaches usually offer an uninterrupted horizon, making them ideal for potent morning sunlight. The reflection off the water can also amplify the benefits you receive.
2. **Mountain High**: Being at a higher altitude not only offers cleaner air but also a stronger dose of sunshine. The thinner atmosphere filters less UV light, making your sun-soaking more effective.
3. **Field of Dreams**: Open fields and plains offer expansive views and little to no obstruction, making them excellent options for your morning sunshine routine. Plus, the serenity of these places adds a meditative quality to the experience.

Final Thoughts

Whether you're a city dweller with limited options or someone who regularly communes with nature, the key is to adapt your morning sunshine routine to your environment. Each setting requires a tailored approach, but with a little creativity and planning, you can ensure you're getting the most out of your morning rays, wherever you are.

Travel and Vacation: Keeping Your Morning Sunshine Routine Intact Around the Globe

Traveling offers a break from the mundane, a chance to explore new cultures, and an opportunity to recharge. However, it can also disrupt established routines, including your vital morning sunshine ritual. But worry not—maintaining your routine on the go is achievable with a bit of foresight and planning.

Travel Tips for Sunshine Seekers

1. **Do Your Homework**: Even before you set foot on the plane, make use of online resources to scout out ideal locations for your morning sun-soaking at your destination. Look for parks, beaches, or hiking trails that are easily accessible from your accommodation. Some travel forums and wellness blogs might also offer hidden gems unknown to the casual traveler.

2. **Combatting Jet Lag**: Jet lag can be a routine killer. The disruption to your internal clock might tempt you to hit the snooze button rather than catch the early rays. To mitigate this, try to adapt to your new time zone as quickly as possible. You can do this by adjusting your sleep schedule a few days before you leave, or by using apps that offer jet lag coping strategies.

Globetrotting for the Best Morning Sunshine

Sometimes travel can enhance your morning routine by offering exceptional quality of morning sunlight you wouldn't find at home.

1. **Greek Islands**: Known for their crystal-clear skies and resplendent mornings, the Greek Islands can make your morning sunshine routine feel like a divine ritual. Whether you're in Santorini or Mykonos, the mornings are usually clear, providing a sublime sunshine experience.

2. **New Zealand**: From coastal plains to mountainous terrains, New Zealand offers a diverse range of sun-exposure experiences. Whether you're on the beaches of the North Island or in the Southern Alps, the country provides various backdrops to your morning routine.

3. **The Andes**: If you're adventurous, the Andean highlands offer an unmatched purity of morning sunlight due to their high altitudes. The thin atmosphere allows for a more potent UV exposure, so remember your sunscreen!

Wrap-Up

Travel doesn't have to put a pause on your wellness habits. By integrating these travel tips into your planning, you can continue to prioritize your morning sunshine routine, no matter where your wanderlust takes you. The world is full of exceptional locations that can offer a unique and enriching morning sun-soaking experience. Why not make the most of them?

Conclusion

This chapter has equipped you with a range of advanced tips and hacks, from selecting the ideal grounding footwear to finding the best locations for soaking up morning sunshine. Each of these insights is designed to elevate your 10-minute morning ritual, adding layers of convenience, effectiveness, and enjoyment.

The journey toward optimized well-being is a continuous one, filled with opportunities for growth and improvement. As you've learned, even small refinements can result in significant gains. Whether it's switching to grounding footwear for added protection or seeking out a serene beach on your travels for a different sun-soaking experience, each change is a step toward a healthier, happier you.

We encourage you to continue exploring, experimenting, and refining your morning ritual. You've established a strong foundation; now it's time to build upon it for even greater health benefits. Remember, the sky's the limit when it comes to your well-being. Make it a lifelong commitment to always seek better ways to start your day right.

Conclusion: Your Journey to 10 X Health

Reflecting on the Journey

As we come to the end of this transformative guide, it's essential to pause and reflect on the journey you've embarked upon. From understanding the science and benefits behind each of the three pillars—grounding, early morning sunshine, and deep breathing—to implementing them in a quick, 10-minute daily routine, you've come a long way.

We delved into the ideal sequence to synergize the effects of these elements and discussed personalization tips to adapt the routine to different lifestyles and health goals. The guide also equipped you with a 30-Day Challenge framework, imparting the value of consistency and habit formation for long-term benefits. Advanced tips and overcoming obstacles further enriched your toolkit, preparing you for a lifetime of well-being.

Take a moment to celebrate the progress you've made. Perhaps you've noticed improved sleep, lower stress levels, or a newfound sense of peace—these are not small feats. Each day you commit to this practice is a victory, cementing habits that have the potential to elevate your quality of life. Give yourself a pat on the back; you've earned it.

Ongoing Commitment

The Journey Beyond the 30-Day Challenge: Making Lifelong Commitment to Wellness

Congratulations! You've completed the 30-Day Challenge and are well on your way to establishing a routine centered around grounding, morning sunshine, and deep breathing. While the initial challenge was an excellent springboard, true wellness is not a one-time event but a continuous journey. The benefits of these practices compound over time, increasing your overall sense of well-being. Here's how to maintain your momentum and make this 10-minute morning ritual a lifelong habit.

Setting the Stage for Long-Term Success

1. **Utilize Technology for Reminders**: In this digital age, leverage your phone or smart device to set daily or weekly reminders. Applications like Google Calendar or specialized wellness apps can keep you on track.

2. **Synergize with Existing Habits**: The key to forming a new habit is to anchor it to a pre-existing one. For example, make your grounding ritual a part of your coffee-making routine. This coupling makes it easier for the new habit to stick.

3. **A Collective Journey**: Health and well-being are not solitary pursuits. Involve your family members, roommates, or even your social circle in your routine. Not only will this make the journey more enjoyable, but it will also build a sense of accountability among participants.

4. **Stay Agile and Adapt**: Just like everything in life, your needs and circumstances will change. When they do, don't hesitate to fine-tune your routine. Maybe you'll need to switch from morning to evening grounding sessions, or perhaps you'll discover a new form of breathwork that resonates with you. The key is to be flexible while maintaining the core elements that make the routine beneficial.

Why Long-Term Commitment Matters

The power of these practices lies in their cumulative effect. One-off experiences can be impactful, but when performed regularly, grounding, sun exposure, and deep breathing can bring about more profound and lasting changes. It could manifest in better sleep, increased energy, or even a more grounded emotional state.

The transition from a 30-day challenge to a lifetime habit might appear daunting, but remember, you're investing in a future with increased vitality and well-being. With a little foresight and a commitment to adaptability, your 10-minute morning ritual can grow into a cornerstone of a life well-lived.

Building Your Wellness Tribe: The Power of Community in Sustaining a Healthy Lifestyle

Navigating the journey towards better health and well-being can be both enriching and challenging. While personal determination is critical, the support and collective wisdom of a like-minded community can be invaluable in sustaining your efforts. Let's delve into the multi-faceted benefits of community engagement and explore various avenues to find your tribe.

The Benefits of a Supportive Community

1. **Collective Wisdom**: A community often brings together individuals from diverse backgrounds and experiences. This collective wisdom can offer fresh perspectives, additional resources, and solutions to challenges you may encounter.

2. **Accountability**: It's easier to stick to a routine when you know others are watching or expecting you to show up. This accountability can be a powerful motivator on days when your resolve wavers.

3. **Emotional Support**: A community can offer emotional upliftment, celebrating your victories and offering compassion or advice during setbacks.

Finding Your Tribe: Where to Look

1. **Online Forums**: Websites like Reddit are treasure troves of specialized knowledge. Subreddits focused on wellness practices can provide you with both advice and moral support. You can

ask questions, share your experience, and even find a virtual accountability partner.

2. **Social Media Groups**: Platforms like Facebook have numerous groups dedicated to wellness practices. These spaces allow for more in-depth discussions, sharing of articles, and even organizing virtual or in-person events.

3. **Local Meet-Ups**: If you prefer face-to-face interactions, platforms like Meetup.com can connect you with local enthusiasts who share your interests. These meet-ups could be as simple as collective morning rituals in a local park or more structured, like workshops or seminars.

4. **Workshops and Seminars**: Keep an eye on community boards, libraries, or wellness centers for workshops or seminars. These events are not just educational but also offer an excellent opportunity to network with like-minded individuals.

The Ripple Effect: Giving Back to the Community

Participation in a community is a two-way street. As you gain insights and support, there's an opportunity to give back. Whether it's by sharing your own success story, offering tips, or providing emotional support to newcomers, your contribution completes the cycle of positive reinforcement. This communal sharing further strengthens the group and, by extension, boosts your own commitment to wellness.

Community engagement is more than just a supplementary aspect of your wellness journey; it's a catalyst that can significantly enhance the quality and sustainability of your practices. By finding and contributing to a community that resonates with you, you build a supportive network that could be the cornerstone of a lifelong commitment to better health and well-being.

What's Next?

Lifelong Learning in Wellness: Taking Your Education Beyond the Book

While the book you've read serves as an excellent primer for foundational wellness practices such as grounding, soaking up early morning sunshine, and deep breathing, the pursuit of wellness is an ever-evolving journey. It's akin to a garden that flourishes with ongoing care and updated knowledge. Here's how you can keep cultivating your understanding and stay on the cutting edge of wellness.

Deep Dive with Additional Resources

1. **Websites**: There are several platforms offering rich content that delves into the intricacies of wellness pillars. Websites like HealthLine, WebMD, and specialized blogs provide scientific perspectives and user testimonials that can enrich your understanding.

2. **Podcasts**: Audio formats like podcasts can be a convenient way to stay updated. Look for podcasts that feature experts in the field and discuss scientific research, user experiences, and emerging trends.

3. **Academic Journals**: For those interested in a more scholarly understanding, academic journals offer rigorous studies and findings that can add depth to your knowledge. Platforms like PubMed or Google Scholar are good starting points.

Broaden Your Horizons with Books and Courses

1. **Specialized Books**: Beyond introductory texts, there are specialized books that offer deep dives into each wellness pillar. These books often contain not just theoretical knowledge but

also practical exercises, questionnaires, and guidelines for a more tailored experience.

2. **Online Courses**: Websites like Coursera, Udemy, or edX offer courses on wellness practices. These courses often come with video lectures, interactive quizzes, and peer assessments that can provide a classroom-like experience from the comfort of your home.

KEEP YOUR FINGER ON THE PULSE

1. **Newsletters**: Subscribing to specialized newsletters in the field of wellness can provide you with a constant stream of updated information, right in your inbox. These newsletters often summarize the latest research, offer tips, and highlight upcoming events or courses.

2. **Google Alerts**: Setting up Google Alerts for key terms related to your wellness pillars ensures that you never miss out on the latest publications, studies, or discussions in the field.

WHY ONGOING EDUCATION MATTERS

Investing in continuous learning allows you to:

- **Adapt to New Information**: Science is ever-evolving, and what may be considered a best practice today could be updated tomorrow. Being informed allows you to adapt your practices accordingly.

- **Deepen Your Understanding**: Each layer of additional knowledge adds depth to your understanding, making your practice more meaningful and effective.

- **Equip Yourself for Discussions**: Being well-read allows you to actively participate in community discussions, contributing meaningfully and also benefiting from the wisdom of others.

Your commitment to ongoing education in wellness is a commitment to yourself. By actively seeking out new knowledge, you not only enrich your own practice but also contribute to a broader understanding of wellness, benefiting both you and the community you engage with.

Elevating Your Wellness Practice: How to Scale and Experiment with Your 10-Minute Morning Routine

Congratulations on mastering your initial 10-minute morning routine. While this accomplishment sets a strong foundation for your wellness journey, it's just the beginning. Just as an artist starts with a sketch before creating a masterpiece, your basic routine serves as the blueprint for a more refined, intricate wellness regimen. Here's how to take your practice to the next level.

Extend the Canvas: Lengthen Your Routine

1. **Time Allocation**: Consider allocating more time to each component of your morning ritual, such as grounding, sun exposure, and deep breathing. This will allow you to dive deeper into each practice and reap additional benefits. For example, instead of five minutes of deep breathing, aim for ten.

2. **Incremental Increases**: If you're unsure about dedicating more time all at once, you can gradually add extra minutes to each pillar over weeks or months. The key is to listen to your body and adjust accordingly.

Introduce New Colors: Incorporate Additional Elements

1. **Mindfulness Meditation**: This practice can work well in tandem with your current routine, enhancing your mental clarity and focus for the day ahead.

2. **Targeted Stretching**: Specific stretches can wake up your body and may even synergize well with grounding practices, offering a physical as well as mental start to your day.

3. **Seasonal Adjustments**: You could even consider seasonal elements like cold showers in the summer or warm herbal teas in winter, to better align with the natural world around you.

Fine-Tune Your Sketch: Track and Adjust

1. **Mood and Energy Levels**: Maintain a daily log where you note your mood, energy levels, and any other relevant indicators after your morning routine.

2. **Sleep Quality**: Use wearables or apps to monitor your sleep and see how it's affected by changes in your routine.

3. **Data Analysis**: Periodically review this data to make data-driven adjustments to your practice. This ensures that your routine is not just based on how you feel but also on measurable improvements in your well-being.

Create Your Masterpiece: Personalization

1. **Individual Preferences**: While the book serves as a guide, everyone's physiology and lifestyle are different. Don't hesitate to tailor each element to better suit your needs.

2. **Family and Work Life**: If you have children or work commitments that make the original 10-minute routine challenging, look for ways to integrate wellness practices into your family life or work schedule.

3. **Cultural Additions**: You might also wish to include cultural or spiritual elements that resonate with you personally, whether that's a brief prayer, a moment of gratitude, or a family tradition.

The Continuous Journey of Self-Improvement

The 10-minute routine you've mastered is a living, evolving entity. The true magic lies in your ability to scale it, experiment with it, and make it your own. Keep pushing the boundaries of what you thought was possible in your quest for well-being. By doing so, you're not just investing in a better today but also paving the way for a healthier, happier future.

Final Words

As we close this book, let's take a moment to celebrate the incredible journey you've embarked upon. You've not only read through these pages but have also committed to implementing practices that can change your life in the most profound ways—all in just 10 minutes a day. That's no small feat.

Your willingness to take control of your health and well-being speaks volumes about the kind of life you aspire to live—one filled with vitality, clarity, and a deep connection with yourself and the world around you. The practices and habits you've formed or are forming are stepping stones toward that life. But remember, this is just the beginning.

The road to health and well-being is not a sprint but a marathon. Your journey to 10 X health doesn't end as you read this final paragraph. In fact, consider it a brand new start. Continue with the practices, share your story with others, and never stop learning. Your health is worth every effort, every minute, and every morning ritual.

So here is my final call to action for you: take control of your health and well-being, one morning at a time. Make your 10-minute morning routine a non-negotiable part of your day. Embrace the challenges and cherish the victories, no matter how small.

The best time to start was yesterday. The next best time is now.

To your lifelong health and well-being.

Made in United States
Orlando, FL
13 January 2025

57252567R00095